A CATHOLIC TEEN'S GUIDE TO
TOUGH STUFF

Straight Talk,
Real Issues

JIM AUER

Liguori

LIGUORI, MISSOURI

Imprimi Potest:
Richard Thibodeau, C.Ss.R. • Provincial, Denver Province
The Redemptorists

Published by Liguori Publications • Liguori, Missouri
www.liguori.org
www.catholicbooksonline.com

Library of Congress Cataloging-in-Publication Data

Auer, Jim.
    A Catholic teen's guide to tough stuff : straight talk, real issues / Jim Auer.—1st ed.
        p. cm.
    ISBN 0-7648-1104-5 (pbk.)
    1. Catholic youth—Religious life. 2. Christian life—Catholic authors.
I. Title.

BX2355.A92 2004
248.8'3'08822—dc21   2003047644

Printed in the United States of America
08 07 06 05 04   5 4 3 2 1
First edition

CONTENTS

INTRODUCTION

Thank you for calling Pizza World, my name is Alice, will this be for pickup or delivery?"

Pizza World is only a few blocks away, so you tell Alice, "Pickup."

"And what can we get for you this evening?"

"Two large pizzas with extra cheese, pepperoni, sausage, and one half mushrooms on one of them." (One of your friends likes mushrooms.)

"Anything else on the pizzas?"

"Uh...I don't think so."

"How about some shriveled, greasy, grotty bologna?"

"*What?*"

"That's okay, we put some on automatically, it's free, no charge. Your order also comes with a side order of our rancid chicken gristles."

"This is a joke, right?"

"Not at all. The chicken gristles are automatic, too. And *free!*"

"But I don't want any of that last stuff! Not on the pizza, not on the side, not anywhere!"

"Comes with your order. You have to take it. If you want the pizza, you get the grotty bologna and the rancid chicken gristles. Oh—and this week, you also get a tub of our Tar-Flavored Tofu. No charge."

❧

You would have some blunt suggestions on what Pizza World can do with their free stuff and their pizza, too. You're not stuck with Pizza World. You can call another pizza place and get a normal, enjoyable pizza. If you're lucky, you may even have a coupon for $2 off.

But you can't enter a different life and get out of the tough, sometimes nasty, stuff that this life brings you from time to time along with the enjoyable parts. Well, actually, you can and will—but it's called heaven, and it's probably quite some time into the future.

In the meantime, you have to deal with the occasional pieces of grotty bologna on your pizza, and there's no coupon that keeps them from being there. Loneliness, depression, addictions of all kinds (whether one's own or someone else's), being victimized by gossip and exclusion, living with tension and uncertainty in the family, living with violence in our society, sometimes rather close to us…there are all kinds of grotty bologna on our pizzas.

They can eat away at the very thing that, in the end, is precisely what will enable us to get through them: our faith. When a chunk of tough stuff drops into our lives, it's tempting to be upset with God, to think that God has stopped caring, or that we have somehow become unworthy of God's help. If we've created the tough stuff ourselves through our own behavior, it's easy to think that God is angry and has decided to leave us alone to get out of the mess we've created.

But God doesn't change. God is God when we're soaring on clouds of joy, and God is God when we're lying in the pits of pain and confusion. God is the same: unconditional love. *The only thing that changes is our ability to feel that love.* When we don't feel it very strongly, for whatever reason, we have to believe in it; we have to know that it is there. We can choose to let challenges erode our faith or strengthen it.

That's the first good news about working through tough stuff. We never have to do it alone.

If you've ever had a broken arm that had to be in a cast and a sling for some time, you remember what it was like when the sling and cast were taken off. Instead of leaping out of its temporary prison, ready for action, your arm almost went limp. The muscles had become weak because they were never working against any resistance.

That's the second piece of good news about the tough stuff of life. It leads to growth. Working through challenges, combating demons both outside and inside us...that's what makes us really grow. "No pain, no gain" may not always be literally true. But "no challenge, no growth" definitely is. The mistake is thinking that problems and mountainous challenges will always drag us down, or that there's something wrong with us when we experience them.

Maybe you'll experience more than what seems like your due share of unfair situations, huge challenges, and difficult decisions as you move toward adulthood. Maybe less. Maybe you'll find it harder than others to keep the rules of good moral behavior, and maybe you'll have an easier time of it. There's a certain mystery about the way life comes at us, both from outside and from within ourselves. And the same situation or decision that doesn't even qualify as a problem for one teen can be a mountain for another. As we often say, "Go figure."

But this much is true for all of us: The more time and energy we spend thinking about how unfairly difficult something is, the less time and energy we have left to work through it.

Words From the Word

My child, when you come to serve the Lord, prepare yourself for testing.

Sirach 2:1

We know that all things work together for good for those who love God, who are called according to his purpose.

Romans 8:28

Other Voices

The problem is not that there are problems. The problem is expecting otherwise and thinking that having problems is a problem.

Theodore Rubin

God gave burdens, also shoulders.

Yiddish proverb

The will of God will not take you where the grace of God cannot keep you.

Anonymous

Bottom Line

Tough stuff is a part of life. It doesn't usually feel good, but in the end—in some way or other—it can work *for* good. A person of faith never has to face it alone.

ONE
LIVING ON LONELY STREET

I am like an owl of the wilderness, like a little owl
of the waste places.

Psalm 102:6

❦

found a new place to dwell. It's down at the end of
Lonely Street at Heartbreak Hotel...I get so lonely I
could die." If you listen to Oldies, you may recognize
these 1956 lyrics from Elvis. But loneliness goes back
much further than the birth of rock and roll.

"Look on my right hand and see—there is no one
who takes notice of me; no refuge remains to me; no one
cares for me." The writer of Psalm 142 wrote those words
nearly three thousand years ago. Loneliness isn't new.

It's not rare, either. According to one survey, one-
fourth of all adults feel deeply lonely every few weeks.
The rate among teens and young adults is higher. If you're
lonely, you're not alone.

Loneliness isn't *being* alone; it's *feeling* alone. You
can feel lonely when a couple hundred people in a school

cafeteria surround you, even if several of them are friends who are talking with you.

Loneliness is feeling *disconnected* from others, or from someone in particular who is very important to you. Being connected with other people is one of the deepest needs we have. Happiness shared is doubled; sorrow shared is cut in half. Even ordinary events in our lives, things that are neither exceptionally joyful nor painfully sad, feel incomplete when there's no one to relate them to.

Loneliness is tough to handle, and it gets tougher if you conclude that it means something is wrong with you. The rest of the human race seems to be out having a good time, enjoying healthy relationships, happily sharing their lives...and then there's lonely (and therefore, defective) you. That's the way it *feels*; that's not the way it *is*.

It's like this. If you have an ache in your shoulder, does that mean something is wrong? Technically, yes. Pain is the body's way of saying, "Something has happened that needs attention." If the pain continues for days or weeks and gets worse, then obviously there's a condition or an injury that needs treatment.

But you don't call 911 every time your shoulder aches—or your head or your back. It's the same with your heart and your feelings. No one goes through life without ever getting a headache—or heartache and feelings of loneliness. It doesn't mean a drastic condition is about to ruin you if it's not fixed within the next couple of days.

Life is a rhythm. There are times your shoulder will

feel like it could set a shot-put record, and there are times when it will ache. There are times when you'll feel happy, fulfilled, and accepted, and times when you'll feel lonely. It's not fun, but it's definitely not abnormal.

The first thing to do if you're lonely may sound strange: Admit to yourself that you're lonely. Many people don't want to face their loneliness. They'd prefer to think of it as something else, especially if they see it as a fault or a defect. But honestly telling yourself "I'm lonely" is much healthier than saying "I get bad breaks" or "Everybody around me is self-centered and snobby."

Now expand that statement: "I'm lonely—*and it's OK!*" That doesn't mean it feels good, doesn't mean you'll stay that way, doesn't mean you're accepting a state of hopelessness. You're simply affirming the truth that, even when lonely, you are not weak or defective; you're normal.

The next step may seem weird, and maybe it doesn't always apply to you, but ask yourself if you truly want to change your loneliness. It's possible to prefer being lonely over actively trying to change it.

For one thing, staying lonely is easier. Not more fun, just easier. Working through any problem, including this one, is just that—work.

Second, loneliness can be oddly appealing. It can seem romantic and beautiful in a sad way. There are tons of poetry, some good and some really bad, which can reinforce that impression and help you hold on to loneliness, even when there's an opportunity to feel otherwise.

("No, I can't go anywhere with you. I'm busy reading

about how the sun shines but not for me, and birds are singing but I can't hear them, and then I'm going to write my own sad, sweet poem about the gray clouds of cruel fate pouring acid rain on the helpless, fragile, dying garden of my shattered hopes and dreams.")

Loneliness can invite phony "cures" that are actually traps. They all have this in common: They *seem* like they'll fix the problem or at least relieve some of the hurt. But none of them is a cure. Some may relieve the hurt for a short while, but the relief is temporary and eventually brings even more hurt. It's like taking strong medication to temporarily relieve that ache in your shoulder, but the medicine soon causes more pain in your gut than the ache in your shoulder...which is still there.

Psychoactive substances are an obvious false cure. Several cans of beer or a couple of joints never made anyone less lonely. Drunk, high, or stupid, but not less lonely.

A daily endless string of TV shows, video games, or computer games is another trap. They're fine when they provide a legitimate break from work, but they fail miserably when they're used to cope with loneliness. The same is true of hours and hours on the Internet.

Trying to reverse loneliness by jumping into a frenzy of activity—joining one thing after another, taking on one task after another—doesn't work either. There's not enough time to feel really connected with all of them (feeling disconnected is the problem, remember), and you end up basically just stressed.

Trying to establish a very close friendship or romantic

relationship *very quickly* is still another loser, particularly if it becomes possessive. Finding an understanding, supportive friend is a wonderful gift from God. But seeing that person as a personal salvation from loneliness, and demanding exclusive attention is misusing the gift.

Sex as an attempted cure for loneliness will make it worse. It *seems* to promise the very things a lonely person needs: acceptance, sharing, intimacy, and love. But sex by itself doesn't deliver any of those things, and soon it becomes obvious that it was only sex...lonely, meaningless, wasted sex.

You can actually make loneliness work *for* you. Not that you should think, "I'm lonely—what a lucky break! Let's hope this lasts!" No, let's hope loneliness lasts only long enough to have a positive effect. Here are some opportunities that it can provide.

1. *A time to fill the heart.* The most memorable line from a musical called *The Fantasticks* contains a golden truth about human nature: "Without a hurt, the heart is hollow." A person with a hollow heart doesn't know how to give support, comfort, compassion, or consolation to others because he or she has seldom felt those needs, or has tuned them out. Someone who has experienced loneliness and coped with it is far better able to reach out to others who are hurting. If you've seldom suffered a scratch, you have a hard time identifying with someone who is bleeding all over.

   Times of loneliness are opportunities to fill your heart with empathy for people who will need it from you. You, including the loneliness you've felt, will be God's gift to them.

2. *A time to rediscover simple wonders.* We tend to forget about simple things when we're busily involved with other people, but they're among the riches of life. Some examples are watching a bird in flight; appreciating the incredible complexity of a flower's blossom; feeling the breeze flow across your body as you walk somewhere by yourself, noticing what's on and around the path or the sidewalk; being aware of your own breathing; noticing color, wherever it is.

3. *A time to learn about yourself.* Times of being alone—and perhaps lonely—are opportunities to look deeply inside ourselves and discover things we might miss when life is a flurry of interaction with others.

   Loneliness can be a great thought-starter and the occasion of making valuable lists: "Things I Really Believe," "Goals I Want to Accomplish," "One Hundred Good Things About Myself," and "One Hundred Things I'm Grateful For (in spite of being lonely)."

4. *A time to reconnect with God.* It can be easy to let God slip into the background of our lives when we're caught up in many activities and feeling great about everything. Loneliness can jog us back into contact.

   Don't be afraid that God will greet you with, "WELL…! This is just *great!* Now that you don't have a lot of other people in your life, you finally come to *me!*" God might have a legitimate complaint there, but there's no evidence that he makes it. If *you* desperately loved someone and that person came (back) to you and wanted to be with you, would you turn your back on him or her? No, you'd be overjoyed at the return. So is God.

Whatever the cause of loneliness, the cure is no mystery. It's you. That may sound simple and a bit too cute, but it's basically true.

So bake a cake.

Yes, bake a cake. If you don't know how, buy two or three cake mixes—they're not expensive—and learn. If you're a guy, recall that real guys bake cakes, and some of them even make big bucks doing so. For an extra kick, turn white icing into bright orange by adding red and yellow food coloring. (Go easy on the red.)

Then give this cake to somebody, even if it's the next-door neighbors you haven't had a conversation with in eighteen months. Enjoy the look on their faces. Or invite somebody over to help you eat it.

It doesn't have to be baking a cake. *Do something different and good*—something that gets you out of yourself and preferably involves other people on the receiving end of your effort and generosity. It can be joining the stage crew when the drama teacher puts out a plea for help, getting involved in the canned food drive, or volunteering for almost anything. (Remember to choose one activity, maybe two, but not twelve.)

You have to take that first uncomfortable step out of your situation and into initially unfamiliar territory. Otherwise, you're stuck with your *familiar* territory...which is lonely.

Mother Teresa wrote, "When Christ said 'I was hungry and you fed me,' he didn't mean only the hunger for bread and for food; he also meant the hunger to be loved. Jesus himself experienced this loneliness. He came among his own and his own received him not, and it hurt him then and it has kept on hurting him. The same hunger, the same loneliness, the same having no one to be accepted by and to be loved and wanted by. Every human being in that case resembles Christ in his loneliness, and that is the hardest part; that's real hunger."

Reach out to someone else who is lonely. It shouldn't be too difficult to find a lonely person. Maybe it's a peer, a classmate who has difficulty fitting in and making friends. Maybe it's a grandparent who lives alone.

Make contact. Suggest an activity. If the person lives some distance away, call, e-mail, or send a card. Better yet, *make* and send a card, with a letter tucked inside. (Leave the topic of your loneliness out of the letter.) If you're not certain whom to contact or what to suggest, pray over it and expect an answer. God is not going to turn down an offer from someone to help someone else. Rising out of your loneliness while helping someone out of his or hers is a double winner.

No one wants to deliberately invite loneliness, but remember that we usually learn our most valuable lessons and experience our deepest growth during sad times from which we emerge stronger, deeper, better. "Without a hurt, the heart is hollow."

Words From the Word

He turns a desert into pools of water, a parched land into springs of water.

Psalm 107:35

Other Voices

If there were no tribulation, there would be no rest; if there were no winter, there would be no summer.

Saint John Chrysostom

If you want the rainbow, you gotta put up with the rain.

Dolly Parton

Bottom Line

A normal human being, living a normal, balanced life, will still get lonely at times. It's OK—and you can turn it into an opportunity.

TWO

WHEN THE BLUES DON'T GO AWAY

O Lord, why do you cast me off? Why do you
hide your face from me?

Psalm 88:14

❧

'm depressed," one of my students growled one day
after classes. "Look at this!" He opened his assign-
ment book to the current date. It was pretty well filled
with notes and page numbers. I looked at it.

"You're not depressed," I said matter-of-factly.

"I guess you think all this homework is going to be
fun?"

"Can't comment on the fun factor," I said. "As a
teacher, I'm probably supposed to say it looks like a great
time, but I won't do that. In any case, you're not depressed."

"I'm not?"

"No, you're…" and at that point I used a common,
colorful word that means upset and angry. I've forgot-
ten exactly what it was.

There's a big difference between suffering from genuine, continuing depression and simply being upset, sad, angry, sorry for yourself, or having a bad day or even a bad week. Those aren't fun things either, and sometimes, not always, you could call them temporary, short-term depression.

Many things can cause that—the death of a friend or relative, the breakup of a relationship, a failure at school, in athletics, or in making friends. Even hormones. Now it's easy, especially for adults, to take any adolescent difficulty or mood swing and say, "Hormones…as usual… goes with the territory." It's not that simple; but still it *is* true that the swirl of hormones during adolescence can cause big mood swings, especially downward. And since hormones don't announce ahead of time, "We are now swinging into action, so prepare for a huge dip in the road," it can be frustrating to feel down and not have a clue as to why.

But here we're talking about blues that really don't go away. The down feelings go on for days and weeks. During that time, you have little or no ambition or energy for most of the things you used to do. Activities you used to enjoy now seem dull and hardly worth doing. ("Let's check out the mall." "Nah." "Why not?" "Don't feel like it.")

You feel tired almost all the time, no matter what. It doesn't matter if you get five hours sleep or fourteen hours sleep; you still wake up tired. It doesn't matter if you work hard twelve hours a day or vege out on the couch watching Cartoon Network twelve hours a day; you're

tired in both cases. You may have difficulty going to sleep
or difficulty staying asleep, or you may sleep almost end-
lessly; you're still tired.

Little irritations seem enormous. Not having enough
milk for cereal in the morning takes on almost the same
disaster status as getting a D-minus on the final exam
when you needed at least a C to pass the course. Almost
anything that goes wrong makes you feel, *"I don't need
THIS too!"*

You find it hard to concentrate, focus, decide, or remember. Tasks that normally take forty-five minutes now
consume hours, and they're still not done completely or
well. Writing a two-page paper feels like writing a book.
Everything feels like a mountain. It takes a huge effort
just to start anything, and five minutes into it, you want
to take a break.

In really serious cases, nothing matters. Nothing. If
you find you're failing four out of six classes, it's not
much different than if you find out the temperature is
four degrees below normal outside. It just doesn't matter. If you lose every privilege—going out, TV, phone,
computer, CD player, video games—it doesn't matter. You
no longer enjoy most of those things very much anyway.

You feel like a failure in spite of past, maybe even
fairly recent, success. You may even turn it around and
decide to "succeed" by almost deliberately failing at things.

You may even consider suicide. That's a biggie, and
we'll talk about it in a chapter all its own, coming up
next.

Throughout all this is the feeling that either God

doesn't care (just as you may not care about anything), or that you're not a very good person because if you were, God would do something to make you happy because he loves you. Hearing a hymn verse like "He will hold you in the palm of his hand" either makes you want to puke or feel "Yeah, well, that works for good people, normal people, holy people—God likes *them.*"

Like most other life conditions, there are many degrees of depression. A depressed person may experience only some or all of the above symptoms, and in varying degrees. It's somewhat like a cold: sometimes you just sniffle frequently, and sometimes you sneeze like a volcano every ten minutes and feel like your nasal passages are stuffed with concrete.

It's worth noting that many of the above signs of depressions are identical to the signs of marijuana addiction. That makes a lot of sense, actually. Someone who regularly needs weed in order to feel that life is worth living is likely to feel at least somewhat depressed when he or she isn't high. And then the result feeds and reinforces the cause. A joint or two seems to relieve depression.

Basically, there are two major causes of depression, often called chemical and situational. You might think of them in terms of inside and outside. In the former, there literally is an imbalance of normal body chemistry. The body produces many natural chemicals. Some, like adrenalin, spur us to action when we are challenged, threatened, or frightened. Others, such as endorphins, give us a feeling of well-being, a feeling that life is good and worthwhile and fun. When they're not running around in the right proportions, it can have consequences on how we feel about life and about ourselves.

This type of depression is particularly maddening because you search for a reason and can't find one. Neither can anyone else. Most of the things in your life may be going rather well. From all the evidence, you're normal, healthy, reasonably successful, and you have lots of things to be thankful for...but you still feel down.

Now don't jump to hasty conclusions. If you're feeling a little down for a couple days or so for no apparent reason, don't decide, "My body chemistry must be really screwed up." True chemical depression is not as common as the common cold.

The other kind of depression, situational, results from an event or series of events that involve some kind of major change or loss; often the same event can cause both change and loss. Being uprooted from school and friends when the family moves can do it easily. The breakup of a family through divorce is a huge change and loss, even if home life is more peaceful without the arguing and fighting that preceded the divorce.

The loss of a loved one is another obvious cause. This can happen in many ways, ranging from death to the breakup of a relationship. Keep in mind, though, that a certain period of grieving—feeling the pain of loss—is not only normal but also *necessary* to recover from the loss. Trying to convince yourself that you don't really hurt very much, that things are really pretty cool anyway, actually prevents recovery. But normal grieving is not the same as depression. It can *lead* to depression if a person gets stuck in it and never works through it. But in general, normal grieving is healthy; genuine depression is not.

What do you do about genuine depression? Two things: get help, and learn to help yourself. Let's take those one at a time.

Serious depression may require help from somebody to get through. It is true that depression sometimes does fade away after a while. But if it doesn't, getting help may be a necessary step. Even if it will, a little assistance can shorten the duration.

Unfortunately, "getting help" has a bad image, thanks to sometimes sarcastic or even playful remarks, such as "Man, you need help," which suggest sickness and weakness. But seeing a counselor does not mean you're a weak person, unable to handle life the way you "should" if you were "normal." It can be a strong, intelligent thing to do.

If your golf stroke is getting really off, you get help from a coach or a pro. If your body is seriously injured, you go to doctor, and then when it's recovering, to a physical therapist. If your algebra or calculus grade is borderline, you ask for extra help from the teacher or an adult or peer tutor.

Somehow we do all kinds of things like that without thinking we're weak, substandard people. Well, getting help in just dealing with life in general (which can be harder than recovering from a specific injury) doesn't make us weak, substandard people either.

Of course, you have to *want* help. You have to want

things to change and be willing to make some changes in yourself for that to happen. It's possible, once you realize that you're really depressed, to use that as a crutch. It's even possible to embrace depression because it seems to release you from any obligation other than basically moping around. "I can't be expected to succeed or accomplish anything or even work much at anything—after all, I'm depressed."

Even if you get some people to buy that and excuse you from responsibility, it's a bad trade because your heart and gut will tell you that this is not exactly a formula for making your dreams come true.

There are some things you can do for yourself. A major part of depression is feeling that your life is out of control, and that you're just a little pawn that people and events are pushing around on the chessboard of life.

So do some things that help you feel you're retaking control of your life. Make some decisions and carry them out. It doesn't matter if they're really little ones at first. (Trying to retake total control and solve everything right away can be, well, depressing!) Almost any little decision will work, even if it's not directly related to the cause of depression.

Decide to exercise and do it, even if it's only for ten minutes. It doesn't matter whether it's walking, jogging, aerobics, or stretching. Many people who are subject to depression from time to time, and who know from experience what's going on, will *make* themselves take a walk—and deliberately try to notice pleasant things while they're walking.

If your desk or work area is a disaster of clutter, decide to spend *ten minutes* clearing off a few square inches of it. Make some hard-line decisions about what to keep and what to throw away with no regrets. After ten minutes, stop because you've made progress...unless, by that time, you're on a roll and really feel like going further.

The key is to make a decision—one that's very doable—and go through with it. Feeling a little more in control of something, no matter what, is a lift. It doesn't solve the whole depression thing, but it does give you a lift, and that's what you need. Just make sure it's something *in your own life* that you're gaining control of. It's easy to substitute something in somebody else's life. "If I can make my bratty little brother stop being bratty, I'll feel better." That doesn't work because, once again, your heart and gut will tell you that, even if the little brother becomes an instant angel, *your* life and situation haven't changed.

As we noted some time ago, real depression affects our relationship with God. We may feel God doesn't notice; God doesn't care; I'm too defective for God to help or even want to help; God may be trying to help, but I'm too defective to know how to receive it; God may be planning to help sometime in the future, but I just don't have it to wait until then; where is all this joy that's supposed to come from believing in Jesus? I don't see it or feel it, so maybe this whole faith thing isn't for real, maybe it's just a joke; now I feel guilty about doubting that it's real...and that's depressing.

Well, you're not defective, and you have company.

Let's start with Jesus himself. "My God, my God, why have you forsaken me?" (Matthew 27:45; Mark 15:34). Yes, he was physically suffering immensely on the cross, but physical suffering isn't the only kind, and he obviously felt emotional and spiritual abandonment as well.

Then let's go to the writer of Psalm 88, which is both a cry for help and a cry of anger coming from the pits of depression. It screams out pain and even resentment against God. Apparently, God can handle this because he inspired its writing.

Then let's go to saints, who seemed to suffer from depression of one kind or another. Saint Jerome, Bible scholar and holy as he was, was also described as frequently morose and in a bad mood. Saint John of the Cross wrote a spiritual classic about "the dark night of the soul" when he felt painfully distant from God, even though he wanted to feel close to God and okay about himself.

Feeling down? You're in good company.

Get out a Bible, look up Psalm 88, and pray it. Feel it. Mean it. And know that you are heard.

Words From the Word

If I go forward, he is not there; or backward, I cannot perceive him; on the left he hides, and I cannot behold him; I turn to the right, but I cannot see him. But he knows the way that I take; when he has tested me, I shall come out like gold.

Job 23:8–10

Come to me, all you that are weary and are carrying heavy burdens, and I will give you rest.

Matthew 11:28

Other Voices

In happiness, iron is bright; in sadness, gold is dull.

Ontario proverb

Toil on, sad heart, courageously,
And thou shalt find thy dream shall be
A noonday light and truth to thee.

Ellen Sturgis Hooper

If you were happy every day of your life, you
wouldn't be human. You'd be a game show host.

Winona Ryder in the film Heathers

Bottom Line

Everyone has a bad, down day, even a bad, down week
or more. Real depression is much bigger than that. But it
really *isn't* the end of the world no matter how much it
feels like it. Not with God on your side.

THREE

WHEN SUICIDE SEEMS LIKE AN (ATTRACTIVE) OPTION

But [Elijah] went a day's journey into the wilderness, and came and sat down under a solitary broom tree. He asked that he might die.

1 Kings 19:4

On that day [Sarah] was grieved in spirit and wept. When she had gone up to her father's upper room, she intended to hang herself. But she thought it over...

Tobit 3:10

❧

Suicidal thoughts in people in the Bible? Yes. There they are, right above.

I was once talking with a teen who had a lot in common with Elijah and Sarah. We were in my classroom where he had come to see me after school. I had taught him a couple years previously. A few days ago, he had made a half-serious attempt at suicide.

I decided to be very blunt.

"Well," I said, "if you do away with yourself, you'll never get to make love to a beautiful woman who's spending her life with you. And you'll never hear a little kid call you 'Daddy.' Personally, I think both of those are too good to miss."

Lovemaking is better than suicide? Yeah. Actually, everything is. It just may not seem like it at the time.

Nearly five thousand young people between the ages of fifteen and twenty-four take their lives each year. Suicide is the third-leading killer of people in that age group.

This chapter includes three parts: (1) if a friend has already taken his or her life; (2) if you think or know that a friend is considering suicide; and (3) if *you* have considered it. If the third possibility applies to you, go right to that section now. It's clearly marked, and it's also blunt.

If a Friend Has Committed Suicide

If that has happened recently, some hymns may make you want to rip up the hymn book when you hear them. "And hold you, hold you in the palm of his hand." "Be not afraid. I go before you always." You feel like saying, "Yeah, right, God. Who writes your hymn lyrics—the same people who write headlines for supermarket tabloids?"

Your anger toward God over a friend's suicide may not be quite that sarcastic, but anger and frustration usually rule for a while, along with shock and pain. When someone you know commits suicide, at first you feel like you've been slugged in the gut with a sledgehammer.

Then come the questions. "Why?" "How could God let this happen?" They surface every few minutes at first and hang around for quite some time.

You yourself may question things that used to seem obvious, even though you didn't think about them constantly—very basic things, such as "God has a plan for each of us," "Life has meaning," "God loves and cares for each of us," and even, "There is a God." Suddenly those things don't *feel* so certain after all. And when people say something like "Everything happens for a reason" or "Somehow it was God's will," you want to slap them across the room.

Accept your anger and your questioning. God does. God can handle them. They're normal, and so are you for having angry feelings and questions. But don't get stuck with them forever. Get some help resolving them. Talk them out.

A feeling of some kind of responsibility is normal too, a feeling that you should have seen it coming, should or should not have said or done this or that—and thus somehow have prevented the tragedy. A single gloomy look that you remember seeing on the person's face can seem like a clear and obvious sign of suicidal thoughts that you were clueless about.

But feeling guilty does not mean you *are* guilty. Now, if your friend had said, "I'm going to kill myself tonight" and showed you the gun, the razor, or the bottle pills, and you simply went home and watched the late show, then, yes, you can legitimately feel some guilt.

But that's almost never the case. Some people show

outward signs of suicidal thoughts (we'll list them in the next section), but other suicides among younger people are impulsive acts, often prompted or aided by the influence of alcohol or other drugs. Walking around slumped over with guilt does neither you nor your departed friend any good.

You may worry also about your friend's fate and wonder, "What has happened to him or her? How did God react to the suicide?"

God probably reacted the same way you did but even more intensely. God is extremely sad over it and angry at whatever conditions prompted it. (God can feel many different things at the same time.) But is your friend doomed? After all, isn't it seriously sinful to deliberately take any human life except in necessary self-defense?

But to be fully guilty of something, a person must be able to make a completely free choice about it. Most medical and religious experts agree that to do something as drastic as ending one's own life, a person has to be burdened by considerable stress and/or depression. That would make him or her less accountable.

The *Catechism of the Catholic Church* clearly states, "Grave psychological disturbances, anguish, or grave fear of hardship, suffering, or torture can diminish the responsibility of the one committing suicide. We should not despair of the eternal salvation of persons who have taken their own lives. By ways known to him alone, God can provide the opportunity for salutary repentance. The Church prays for persons who have taken their own lives" (#2282, 2283).

In the end, you simply have to turn this over to the wisdom and love of God. God is love, and nothing stops that. Nothing. God is also known as light. Think of it like this: Your friend somehow was blinded to that loving light and therefore perhaps gave up on it.

That doesn't mean the light stopped shining on him or her.

If You Think a Friend May Be Considering Suicide

Here are some very general basics.

Suicide is almost always linked to depression, which itself is linked to some kind of change or loss and produces a feeling of helplessness and hopelessness. Seriously depressed people feel they've lost control of their lives, and that their lives are spinning ever downward into further pain and meaninglessness. Suicide seems to offer a way of taking control and ending what feels like a hopeless, intolerable situation.

Common "intolerable" situations include living in a seriously dysfunctional, abusive family; failing to achieve success and/or popularity in school; being saddled with a history of bad decisions that seem to cripple the future; and realizing that one *really is* helplessly addicted to alcohol or other drugs. Those reasons are common to both teens and adults.

Other reasons are more particular to young people. Suicide may seem like the only certain way to gain attention when they feel neglected, unappreciated, and just plain unnoticed by others, whether family, friends, or peers in general.

Still another motive among young people is to punish one or more persons by whom they feel betrayed or rejected. Often this is a former boyfriend or girlfriend. Sometimes it's people in general.

Many, though not all, suicides are thought about ahead of time. Sometimes they are even carefully planned. Along the course of that, the suicidal person may show some signs of this plan.

Some of the most common are loss of interest in regular activities; drawing away from friends; talking about death or suicide, even in an apparently lighthearted way; making remarks that life is stupid and nothing is worthwhile; making shadowy threats, such as "They'll find out," again even in an apparently lighthearted way; suddenly turning into a volcano of anger or resentment; writing about death or drawing pictures or symbols of it; giving away important possessions; suddenly seeming happy and relieved after a long period of being down. Any of these is more significant if it happens shortly after a rejection by a boyfriend or girlfriend or by a significant failure of some kind.

Don't see suicidal intentions every time a classmate sheds some tears over a failed test or a relationship breakup. But don't ignore definite signs, either. *Tell somebody.* Tell a trusted adult and get an indication that this adult takes you seriously and is going to do something. If you get the feeling that the adult thinks your concern is groundless, tell another.

And if a friend mentions suicide, never promise not to tell anyone. If you do, break that promise *immediately*. A promise that endangers someone's life is not a promise to be kept.

If You Have Considered Suicide

As I said, I'm going to be very blunt. Sorry, there's no other way.

According to studies, 20 percent of high school and college students have at some time considered suicide. So if the idea has crossed your mind, you're obviously neither a one-of-a-kind weirdo nor the only depressed, problem-burdened person in the world. Also, if you are really determined to end your life, no one can stop you.

I'm not going to tell you, "Don't kill yourself because God loves you," because either you don't believe that or you believe it but it doesn't seem to help. (It might be good to remember God is bigger than you, and you can't stop God from loving you just by thinking that he doesn't.) However, here are some things to think about. They're all true, whether you like hearing them or not.

There are 11.1 suicides per 100 thousand people in the age bracket of fifteen- to twenty-four-year-olds. If 20 percent have considered suicide, that amounts to 20 thousand young people. But only eleven actually did it.

That means the other *19,989* decided not to or were not successful in the attempt, and they must be glad about that because they're still living. You don't hear anyone later in life saying, "Gee, I wish I had committed suicide back when I was young." But you *will* hear lots of them saying, "Thank God I didn't do it when I was thinking of it." Maybe you should think hard about that testimony.

Killing yourself isn't going to make anyone love you or understand you, in case that's your reason. If they're clueless and unloving while you're alive, they'll be clueless and unloving after you're dead. And even if your suicide did change them, what good would it do *you?* You're not going to lie in a casket thinking, *"Finally* somebody understands and cares." Dead people don't think.

If you're trying to punish someone by ending your life—as in the case of a boyfriend or girlfriend who dumped you—that won't work either. They'll be shocked, sure, but they're much more likely to consider you stupid than to wish they had stayed with you.

Committing suicide to punish someone is always a failure because it punishes the people you *don't want* to punish. The people who genuinely love and care about you will be miserable for a long, long time. But the betraying boyfriend or girlfriend or the nasty classmates? They'll be shocked for a little while, and then they'll get on with their lives and probably end up happy. You won't have a life to get on with. Really bad trade.

To get attention? Well, that'll work for a day or two. It might even make a newspaper headline if you do it in public. But then it'll be over. And you won't know how much, if any, attention you got.

Are you getting the picture? *Suicide really ends.* It's not merely stepping behind the scenes of your life and hiding there while you get satisfaction out of watching everybody on stage go nuts for a little while.

You already know that most suicides are closely linked with depression. But do you also know that most bouts of depression end by themselves in about a year—and even sooner with medication and/or counseling? What a waste it would be to cut short what would have been seventy to eighty years of life because you couldn't wait six months or so to feel better when you were sixteen.

Did you know that many severely depressed people who decide to commit suicide suddenly experience peace and become cheerful and happy? It's true; they do. But *hey*—weren't they going to kill themselves because they thought peace and happiness were impossible for them? Obviously, they were wrong about that.

You may be by yourself when you commit suicide, but you're not alone. Committing suicide is like strapping a bomb to your body and setting it off while surrounded by the people closest to you. You die, but shrapnel flies off and hits them, causing pain and injury beyond imagining, sometimes even resulting in permanent emotional disability. Are you certain you want to do that to people who care about you?

And if you're still determined to take your life, at least do something nice at the end. Find another lonely person and cheer him or her up, brighten his or her day, give him or her something to laugh and be happy about. Bake some cookies, bring them to somebody, and share them. Take a little kid to lunch. Wouldn't that be a nice way to end things? *Just do it* before you go, OK? I dare you. See if it doesn't give you something to think about.

Oh, and yes, God does love you. Sorry, but you can't stop that. If you stick around for a while, you'll feel it.

Ask any of those 19,989 young people who ended up staying alive.

By the way, you might also want to talk to somebody. Try God. Or try God through someone in the phone book. Call 1-800-SUICIDE (784-2433), or look up a suicide crisis center in your area. God's there too.

That's it. I hope you hang around; I really do. So do your future kids and other people you will help and love if you're here.

This isn't just about you, you know.

Words From the Word

My days...come to their end without hope. My eye will never again see good.

Job 7:6–7 (not the end of the story!)

And the Lord restored the fortunes of Job...and gave Job twice as much as he had before.

Job 42:10 (the end of the story!)

Other Voices

Before, I didn't care about living or dying. Now I recognize how beautiful life is.

rapper Napoleon

All I needed was a little faith / So I could catch my breath and face the world again.

Billy Joel, "You're Only Human (Second Wind)"

Believe that life is worth living and your belief will help create the fact.

William James

Bottom Line

No matter how reasonable, necessary, or attractive suicide seems, *it isn't. IT REALLY ISN'T.*

FOUR

THE ALCOHOL LETTERS

Who has woe? Who has sorrow? Who has strife?
Who has complaining? Who has wounds without
cause? Those who linger late over wine...

Proverbs 23:29–30

❦

Those who linger late over wine—or beer or bourbon
or whatever—aren't the only ones, though. They're
not the only ones who have woe and sorrow and strife.
They're not the only ones with reason to complain. The
writers of the following five letters have lots of sorrow
and reason to complain and wounds that didn't have to
be.

None of these letters were actually written. Not on
paper, although they could have been, very easily, and
thousands of times.

Why publish imaginary letters? Because they're not
completely imaginary. These five letters exist in count-
less minds and hearts, and there are many others like
them.

You've almost certainly already been faced with a drinking decision. Whether to or not. At what age. How much. How often. Where, when, under what circumstances.

It all seems so harmless at first, so normal. "Everybody gets hammered now and then." Actually, no, everybody doesn't. But many people do, and the majority of them do not end up in gutters with vomit running down their shirts within a few weeks. Many of them sober up, get themselves to work or to class, and often come out with B averages. The majority of them avoid DUI and vehicular homicide charges. That's what makes it seem so normal, so…safe.

The key word is "seem."

You don't want to become, over the next year, two, ten, or thirty, a person to whom a letter like one of these could be written—whether on paper, or unspoken in the heart of someone you know, love and care about.

One

Dear Dad,

I guess I'd better say here at the start that I love you, and nothing I'm going to say changes that, but I'm afraid that you might think it does. Or that what I'm going to say means I love you less than I would have if things had been different. But then if things had been different, I guess I really would feel at least a little differently about you than I do now. But that doesn't mean…man, I'm getting so confused, I'm not sure I should even go on, but I guess I will.

You did OK. You tried your best with what you were working with. Or maybe I should say with what you were working against. I'm talking about the alcohol. I guess I was maybe nine or ten years old when I first realized that you just plain drank too much. It didn't bother me a whole lot then. I just kind of accepted it and tried to stay out of your way when you were pretty far gone.

You know what I really feel sorry about? That you didn't become the person you could have been. I found out that when you started high school, you were really gifted and athletic, and you had a bright future, a college scholarship probably, maybe even a sports career. But booze killed those things. You barely made it through high school, and you dropped out of college after partying your first year away.

Knowing that makes me sad. Maybe I'm feeling a little sorry for myself too, because we would have had a nicer time of it if you had gotten the jobs you were capable of—or would have been capable of. But mainly I'm sorry for you, for all the things you could have been but weren't because of the alcohol that controlled your life. I still love you, but I just needed to say that I wish things could have been different...for you, for Mom, for all of us.

Two

Dear Mom,

I'm writing this to you because our class is studying this unit on parenthood and family, and I'm feeling two really different things about, well, about you and about me...it's kind of crazy.

First, I want to thank you for carrying me and giving birth to me instead of having me aborted. That probably crossed your mind when you found out that you were pregnant, because I know I sure wasn't planned. It's just that...well, a kid like me is sometimes called a "love child," but now I know that love had nothing to do with it. Alcohol at a no-parents-around party had everything to do with it. It would have been nice to think that I was conceived out of love, even if it wasn't married love. And it would have been nice to have had a father while I was growing up. And it hurts to know that my actual father was a guy who just did it while he was drunk too and that you considered a jerk shortly afterward and from then on.

I feel bad for having these thoughts because it makes me seem ungrateful for life and for what you've done for me, which isn't true. At least I hope it isn't. I'm just really confused right now.

Three

Dear Lisa,

I've gotten along with you better than a lot of kids do with their big sister, and I'm glad about that. We've had some fun times together. Things have changed though. There was a time when I admired you almost like a hero, and there was a time when I could talk with you about anything, which I was grateful for, because you know how Mom and Dad are usually off in their own world.

But it's been a long time since I've felt much admiration, and it's been a long time since we've really talked.

You get hammered almost every weekend and sometimes during the week too. Mom and Dad are clueless, of course, because you've gotten really good at covering it up. As far as I can tell, that's the only skill you've worked at for almost a year. Mom and Dad aren't aware of how much you've changed. They just think you're growing up. I overheard them say something about your going through a stage. I'm not sure if I'm more angry at them or at you.

But besides being angry, I'm a little scared too. A couple of weekends ago, I went to a party at a house where some other clueless parents weren't home. It was a sleepover, and there was lots of stuff available. I figured, what the heck, Lisa does it all the time, and even some of the other girls said, "Hey, your sister Lisa does it all the time." So, I got pretty drunk. Part of me is really ashamed for what I did, but what scares me is that another part of me sort of liked it.

I wish we could talk about it, maybe help each other with it. But if I brought it up, you'd probably congratulate me for growing up and joining the real world, at least as you see it, along with your usual, "Nobody's getting hurt." I don't want to have a problem. The big sister who used to help me with problems now has a big problem herself. I still love you, but I liked you a lot better before.

Four

Dear Joe,

I can't be sure exactly how much guilt you're feeling, but I've known you for seven years—since fifth grade—and I think you're probably drowning in it. I know this probably won't help you much, but I feel guilty too. I was drinking that night just like you were. I didn't get totally hammered, but I sure wasn't thinking too clearly, so I could have done something stupid later on too.

But I'm still out here going to school, driving, hanging out with friends, and sleeping in my own room, while you're locked up, waiting for a hearing. I feel guilty about that because it could have been me in your place. It could have been my life and my parents' lives that drastically changed.

When we drank, we used to joke about how we weren't alcoholics. We told ourselves that we were just normal guys having a good time, and besides we didn't drink all that often anyway, which was sort of true. I feel bad for joking around like that.

One of our teachers said, "It only takes once for alcohol to change your life, and you don't have to be addicted for that to happen." I didn't believe it. I always thought I'd be cool enough not to do anything permanent until I sobered up. Now I feel stupid for having thought that—even though I didn't do any permanent damage that night. I feel rotten that you're the one who's paying the price for both of us having learned that what they said is true.

Five

Dear Alex,

I know it wasn't easy for you when your father and I split up. I'm sorry that things didn't work out between us back then, but there's more to the story than you know. I'm also sorry that things haven't worked out between you and your stepfather because that leaves me torn between two people I love. And I guess I could say that I'm sorry you've been grounded for so long because I like to see you happy and out doing things. But I'm also really tired of being sorry—or maybe the word is *sad*.

You came home late and drunk, or almost drunk, again last night at eighteen years old. I know that you say it's normal and that everybody does it, but I say you're wrong. You say parents don't know what's going on in real life. But what *is* "real life"? Is it getting drunk on weekends? Coming home two hours late with booze on your breath—is that real life?

What about remarrying—after years of struggling as a single mother—and then worrying about a teenage son who is behaving exactly like every other kid who's gotten in trouble with alcohol? Is *that* real life? It's the real life that *I* live. I love you. But I'm also really tired of feeling sorry and sad and worried. I think I deserve a little better.

Alcohol is a huge decision. Whether to or not. At what age. How much. How often. Where, when, under what circumstances. Through your high school and college years, you'll meet hundreds of peers who consider getting under the influence not only normal but the sure way to a good time. But if you look for them, you'll also find a lot of peers who simply don't drink. Which group do you blend in with, or whose behavior do you adopt?

Wrong question. What standards do *you* want for *your* life? How much risky (and, actually, illegal) behavior are you willing to undertake? *That's* the question, and you should answer it yourself.

Unlike some Christian denominations, the Catholic faith has never considered alcohol, in any form and any amount, evil by itself. Jesus himself used wine at the Last Supper when he gave the Eucharist. At his command, we continue to use wine to become his consecrated blood in our Eucharist.

For adults, alcohol by itself is not the point. The point, again, is how much, why, and in what circumstances. A couple of beers at home in front of the TV is one thing. A couple of beers at the stadium when you have to drive a vanload of kids back home is entirely different.

For minors, it's different as well. I could point out that it's illegal and get a *"Really? Tell us more exciting and important stuff we didn't know!"* response, along with a ton of rolled eyeballs and questions about what planet I live on. If you're a party person, in the alcohol sense, and you want to drink, you'll almost certainly find a way to do it, at least now and then.

The point is, alcohol affects a younger body differently than it does an adult body. A person who begins drinking at age fourteen is *four times more likely* to become an alcoholic than someone who begins drinking at the legal age. Fact. Here are some more facts.

- Alcohol kills more people under the age of twenty-one than heroin, cocaine, and all other illegal drugs combined.
- Alcohol is the drug most often used by twelve- to seventeen-year-olds.
- Alcohol-related car crashes are the number one killer of teens.
- Teens who drink six or more days a month are three times more likely to ride in a car driven by someone who has been drinking.
- An estimated eight to ten million underage Americans drink. Approximately one million of them are heavy drinkers.
- One third of all teens think that a can of beer is less powerful than a shot of booze or a five-ounce glass of standard wine. The truth is, they are equal.

Along with those facts, let's take a look at some lies. If they *don't* seem like lies to you, maybe your "real world" and the crowd you hang with isn't really the real world.

- All young people drink.
- All *popular* young people drink.
- Drinking is the only—or at least the best and easiest—way to have a good time.
- Everybody expects you to drink.
- As long as you don't drink a lot every day, or drive when you drink, there's no harm done.
- If you're starting to get dependent on alcohol, you'll have plenty of warning, and you'll be able to stop before anything bad happens.

I hope you make a good decision. You really don't want to receive one of those letters we began with, or a similar one, even if it's not written on paper.

Words From the Word

Wine is a mocker, strong drink a brawler, and whoever is led astray by it is not wise.

Proverbs 20:1

Other Voices

Drunkenness is voluntary madness.

Oregon proverb

Now you live inside a bottle / The reaper's traveling at full throttle / It's catching you but you don't see.

Ozzy Osbourne

The reason I don't drink is that I want to *know* when I'm having a good time.

Nancy Astor

Bottom Line

Alcohol by itself is not evil. But especially for a young person, it's dangerous. Just really dangerous—no matter how "safe" it may seem.

FIVE

TO CHEAT OR NOT TO CHEAT

Bread gained by deceit is sweet, but afterward the mouth will be full of gravel.

Proverbs 20:17

❧

Yes, I do cheat. I just did last evening, and I may cheat again tonight. Okay, I'll even admit that I'm *planning* to cheat tonight because it's supposed to be very cold again, maybe some snow. It's my job to build a fire in the fireplace. Yes, we do own a furnace, but when the weather is cold and snowy outside, leaning on the hearth of a blazing fireplace is much more romantic than sitting on the floor on opposite sides of a heat duct. Builders design them so that they're always behind chairs, sofas, and so on, anyway, and there's nothing romantic about being scrunched between the sofa and a wall.

Traditionally, the man of the house is supposed to create a roaring fire, preferably in the fireplace, starting with only a few scrawny sticks and a single match, *maybe* a little newspaper.

Now I *have* done it that way, but I prefer to cheat. I start with a half dozen of those little immediate-flame fire squares. Then I add some of those wax-filled fire-starter blocks. Then I lay on some fatwood-sticks pressure-saturated with grease and guaranteed to burn fifty feet below the North Pole. I put some real wood on top of that and light it all in several places with a six-inch flame igniter.

That's one form of cheating. Some people might say it's not very adventurous, but nobody would consider it *morally* wrong. But what about cheating that does involve right and wrong?

Of course, you'll have no problem finding lots of people who will say, "I don't think it's really wrong," or at least, "I don't think it's all *that* wrong." You can find people who consider downloading a prepackaged research paper from the Internet simply an intelligent use of available technology. "Hey, it's *technology, man*—you're stupid if you don't take advantage of it!" (There's a nasty assumption that if it's technology, it's okay. But a lot of technology went into the 911 World Trade Center acts of terrorism. Terrorism depends and thrives on it.)

You've seen peers cheating in the classroom or heard them gloating about it afterward. Cheating is all around you and often, very much like alcohol, it's rather easily available. Let's be, well, honest about cheating: it can be extremely tempting.

Where do *you* stand?

A few years ago, the Josephson Institute of Ethics cataloged the responses to several questions asked of almost twenty-one thousand young people across the country.

Of those surveyed, 97 percent said it is important to be a person of good character, and 95 percent of them felt it is important that people trust them. Yet, almost 50 percent of those same young people felt that a person sometimes needs to lie or cheat in order to succeed. Another 41 percent said they would be willing to lie if it would help them get a good job. At the end of the survey, 34 percent admitted that they had lied on one or more of the previous questions. Mr. Michael Josephson, director of the institute that conducted the survey, said, "In terms of honesty and integrity, things are going from very bad to worse."

His comment can be applied to far more than the attitudes and actions of young people. Dishonesty in business has been big news—the Enron fiasco of a couple years ago being only one example.

There are many reasons why some people feel it's okay to cheat. First, as we just noted, many people do it. (Of course, many people commit armed robbery and deal in illegal arms trade, too.) Read almost any edition of any newspaper, and you'll find stories of people who have cheated in business, in politics, in athletics, in almost any field.

Because of that, it's easy to draw two really bad conclusions: (1) Almost *everybody* cheats. (2) Cheating is an acceptable way to achieve a goal—everything is only a game anyway; just don't get caught.

They're both horribly wrong.

1. *Everybody does not cheat.* But the media seldom feature stories of people who achieve something honestly. (How often do you read a story with a lead like "XYZ Corporation *Could* Have Inflated Profits to Lure More Investors But Didn't"? Do you ever see a headline like, "Majority of English 201 Students Say They Could Have Plagiarized But Didn't"?)
2. *God hasn't changed the rules.* There's no new revelation in which God says, "Hey, folks, I realize times have changed. Go ahead and cheat here and there if that's what it takes these days."

Another reason is that we increasingly want to achieve the bottom line quickly, and we tend to skip as many intermediate steps as we can. That's one thing when you're building a fire. It's quite another when you're pursuing a life goal.

We want grades that will produce an impressive diploma that will lead to a good job that will mean a great salary that will bring the cool car and the really nice home. It's even tempting to think we *deserve* all those things just because we were born in this country where they're available—and since we "deserve" them, whatever it takes to get them must be okay, right?

No.

Besides *wanting* success, young people often experience pressure to succeed from parents, peers, and society in general. A firm nudge toward success is good and often needed, but sometimes it pushes people overboard. I've taught kids whose parents considered a single B- on a report card almost the same as an F. Or maybe Dad is an engineer or an attorney, so Dad's kid has to become one too, or something equally high-status. If the kid doesn't think he or she can measure up to that but feels an obligation to do so, cheating to "succeed" can seem like the best way to keep peace at home.

Cheating can also be born of desire and/or pressure to succeed combined with a case of just plain laziness— nothing more psychologically complicated than that. A person wants the good grades to get the good job to get the good salary to get the good stuff...BUT there's, gosh, so much television to be watched and video games to be played and phone conversations to be had and parties to go to and places to hang out. You get the idea.

Even bad time management can be a factor. A month can seem like nearly forever. Suddenly the project or research report that was assigned almost a month ago is due in two days, and that's just not enough time to do it well...and honestly.

Cheating brings two types of consequences. The most obvious is the consequence of getting caught. This in turn brings the disgrace, the punishment, and perhaps the loss of something important and valuable, such as a scholarship or membership on a team. Then comes the difficult job of regaining trust, which can be done only a little at a time. Major cheating is like losing $5,000 out of your bank account on a single bad bet; you have to build it back up $20 and $20 at a time.

Less obvious but probably worse is the consequence of *not* getting caught. Then cheating can become an almost habitual approach to everything, an actual lifestyle. Successfully lifting answers from the test paper on the next desk makes it easier to lift a $20 bill from a wallet or a purse. (Both involve going straight to the bottom line.) This can spill over into relationships as well. ("What a girlfriend or boyfriend doesn't know won't hurt her or him.")

Cheating "successfully" can even become the source of a rush, an addiction that has to be fought almost like alcoholism. I once had a former, usually very successful bank robber (who had long since reformed) speak to my class. A student asked him if he ever felt the urge to pull off one more robbery just for the thrill. "Every morning when I wake up," he answered.

A never-cheat lifestyle brings many rewards. The most immediate, even if it's not the most spiritual, is never having to worry about getting caught. You never have to cover your tracks or wonder if you've covered them well enough. You never have to learn newer, cleverer methods.

You never have to worry about a dishonest act blowing up in your face when it's finally discovered. The newspapers almost daily carry stories of people who finally had to pay for their dishonesty—often (actually, usually) much later, sometimes years later.

You never have to make things seem okay to yourself. People who have adopted cheating as a habitual lifestyle have clubbed their conscience into unconsciousness. But before reaching that stage, they have to rationalize their actions. They have to invent a reason why something that is wrong somehow isn't wrong *this time,* and then try to make themselves believe it.

The first few times, this is pretty easy to do. But after you've told yourself for the fifth or tenth or twentieth time that "it's okay just this once," you hear a voice that says, "You're a liar." Eventually, once cheating has become habitual, that voice will shut up. It's like the alcoholic or drug abuser who comes to believe that getting buzzed almost every day is a perfectly normal, okay lifestyle.

An honest, cheat-free life gives you a huge head start in knowing who you really are because the things you accomplish and obtain are *yours.* They're the result of what *you* did. You can own them and take personal credit for them—after giving thanks for God's gifts. You know they're real, not artificial. You know that what people see when they look at you is genuine, not fake. When someone admires and congratulates you, nothing inside of you dims or extinguishes the nice warm glow you feel.

A lifestyle free of lies and cheating builds a trustworthiness account. This is like a personal but open-to-public-viewing bank account into which you keep making deposits until it's obvious to everyone that you are wealthy. In this case, your wealth is honesty and trustworthiness.

When you really need to be believed, people look at your trustworthiness account and don't hesitate to believe you. When a position requires someone with a large trustworthiness account, your name comes to mind.

Everyone has an account like this, large or small. It's usually open for viewing to friends, family, teachers, and managers. You can prove this to yourself. For example, think of five peers whom you would trust with any-thing—money, a secret, a responsibility, anything. You know which names immediately come to mind. Maybe they're your close friends, maybe not. But you definitely know who is totally trustworthy.

You also know who isn't. They may even be people you basically like and whose company you usually en-joy—but you still wouldn't trust them with anything important.

As a teacher, I've often been asked to write letters of recommendation for students and former students. Ob-viously, I always stress the positives. When they're accu-rate, I cite qualities such as "exceptionally talented," "very energetic," "exhibits strong leadership qualities," and "wonderfully creative," and "goal-oriented."

Sometimes—not always—I also write, "He/she pos-sesses honesty beyond question, a genuine, golden sense of honor. I would, without hesitation, trust him/her to take a final examination alone in a room without being monitored; to keep a crucial piece of confidential infor-mation; or to deliver a large sum of cash *when neither I nor the receiver knows the exact amount,* confident that every cent would get there."

I love it when I can write that about someone.

Words From the Word

The getting of treasures by a lying tongue is a fleeting vapor and a snare of death.

Proverbs 21:6

A good name is better than precious ointment.

Ecclesiastes 7:1

Other Voices

No legacy is so rich as honesty.

William Shakespeare, All's Well That Ends Well

You can't fake quality any more than you can fake a good meal.

William S. Burroughs

Honesty is the first step to greatness.

Illinois proverb

Bottom Line

Cheating can be terribly tempting—and bring terrible consequences, most of which don't show up right away. An honest, cheat-free life gives you a huge head start in knowing who you really are because the things you accomplish and obtain are really *yours*.

SIX

THE SURF CAN TAKE YOU DOWN

You have given them dominion over the works of
your hands; you have put all things under their
feet.

Psalm 8:6

✤

Online host: Ligwriter has entered the room.
Curtainroddle: Oooooo Potz, my friends were just talk-
ing about that last night.
Purplenose1: Anybody here got a pick for the Superbowl?
Skoo18: Hi, Lig.
Ligwriter: Hi, Skoo.
Potzelschnitz: It's all we talk about here too it is sooooooo
cool.
Missortanice: Welcome, Lig.
Ligwriter: Thanks, Miss, and actually, Nose, I do have a
pick but I shouldn't say cuz it'd be bragging.
Online host: Threeoopsio914 has left the room.
Purplenose1: Why bragging, Lig?

Ligwriter: That's, uh, well, because I throw a football for a living.

Curtainroddle: Potz, have you ever seen them in person?

Missortanice: Lig that's awesome. Can you say who you are or at least what team?

Online host: Daddydeckle77 has entered the room.

Purplenose1: Or at least what conference you're in?

Ligwriter: Sorry, better not.

Well, that felt pretty good. Several people acknowledged my existence in a positive way, seemed glad to welcome me into their circle, and apparently accepted the possibility that I'm an NFL quarterback. I think I'm going to stay with these nice folks for a while. After all, when was the last time somebody called my life awesome? A long time—I guess because it isn't exactly awesome. At least I don't feel like it is. And maybe I can flirt a little with Missortanice before I leave the room. Maybe I'll ask her to IM or e-mail me sometime. I could use another friend.

I guess I should be writing a chapter in the book. Trouble is, I don't like the topic: Internet addiction. What do I know about that? It's a boring topic. Being online is ten times more exciting than writing a chapter about Internet addiction. I don't have to get it done right now anyway. Besides, I work better when I'm relaxed and feel good, and being online helps me relax and feel good. When I leave the chat room, I'm going to check out the cool site of jokes and cartoons that I bookmarked this morning. I could use a laugh or two.

The preceding incident didn't happen. But it could have. Living in cyberspace unreality is a daily reality for many people.

You've probably heard the expression "a two-edged sword," referring to something that can hurt you as well as help you. The world is full of two-edged swords. Several decades ago, a now-famous monk, priest, and author named Thomas Merton wrote about them. "Until we love God perfectly, everything in the world will be able to hurt us. And the greatest misfortune is to be dead to the pain they inflict on us, and not to realize what it is."

Merton wrote those words back when computers took up a whole room, were powered by hundreds of vacuum tubes, and weighed over a ton. The Internet didn't exist, hadn't even been dreamed of. But what he wrote could apply to it and to an almost brand-new condition: Internet Addiction Disorder (IAD).

"Addiction" most often brings up images of alcohol and drugs, but we can become addicted to almost anything, even things that are very good in themselves, such as exercise and physical fitness. (A genuine fitness addict who has to miss his or her workout session can get as cranky as an alcoholic locked in a room with nothing but iced tea.)

According to one recent study, over 130,000,000 Americans are online, and thousands more get on each day. The Net has caught on faster than telephones, televisions, and even computers themselves did. But again according to research, about 11 percent of the people going online are becoming compulsive or addicted.

One of the reasons Internet use spread so rapidly is that the Net is basically marvelous. It's a breakaway marvel of technology, an excellent tool, and even a wonderful means of spreading the Gospel, although it can never replace one-on-one sharing of the faith. The pope himself chose the Internet as the theme for World Communications Day on May 12, 2002. He also noted that "the best and worst of human nature" are on display in this third-millennium version of the ancient Roman public forum.

Getting "caught in the net" (the title of an excellent book by Dr. Kimberly S. Young) is particularly easy. The Net is available without much effort and, unlike drugs, it's legal and respectable. It seems foolish not to take advantage of the greatest communication and information vehicle the human race has ever known. In a half hour, you can access data that formerly took several hours or days of research in a library. If you want a pen pal in Ireland or Iceland, you don't have to pay a fee to a snail-mail pen pal service and wait weeks for a name and address. You just click. That part is all good.

But too much of a good thing—even a very good thing—becomes *not* a good thing. Obedience to the Covenant Law in the time of Jesus was a good thing, commanded by God. But some of the Pharisees had gone overboard with it and spent an enormous amount of time fulfilling additions they had made to it. Then they considered all these additions basic religious practice. Nonessentials became essential.

How can you tell if you're using the Net or the Net is

starting to use you? People may be becoming Net-compulsive if they

- feel better when online than at any other time;
- sacrifice sleep to be online;
- cover up or lie about the amount of time they spend online;
- argue with family over the amount of time online and become defensive and angry when someone suggests that it's too much;
- frequently think about and look forward to their next opportunity to go online;
- access sites they don't want anyone else to know about;
- let obligations slide and get online when they should be doing something else (study and homework, for example);
- lie about their age, weight, job, marital status, or gender while in a chat room or pen-palling;
- frequently get online for something brief and simple and discover, when they log off, that they've been online for an hour or two or more.

A person can turn to alcohol to experience feelings that he or she is not getting naturally in real life. A shy guy may find it much easier to talk with a girl when fortified with a couple or so cans of beer. Someone who turns to jelly when confronting another person can find it easy with a couple head start shots of bourbon. Someone who lacks confidence can fantasize dreams of heroic

acts and great accomplishments after a few wine cool-
ers.

In all those cases, the alcohol is "doing the work"—
and that's exactly the point. The alcohol is at work, not
the person. The person is just as shy, confused, bored, or
unconfident as ever.

The Internet can provide the same kind of "assistance." A shy guy can flirt online and never have to worry
about his appearance or in-person social skills. A timid
person who is scared to death of face-to-face confrontations can flame someone else in a chat room and then
leave feeling brave. A person who is too lazy or afraid to
undertake a real-life project can become a conquering
hero playing a computer fantasy game.

This is not to say that meeting people in chat rooms
or playing Internet fantasy or strategy games are un-
healthy in themselves. The crucial point is whether the
Internet is *taking the place of real-life experiences.*

You can learn online, have fun online, even "escape"
online in a legitimate, controlled way, just as you would
watching a movie or a sitcom. But you can't develop
into a mature, responsible, in-charge-of-your-life person
online. That takes real-life, person-to-person, in-the-flesh,
getting-the-job-done experiences.

In Chapter Three of Genesis, Adam and Eve believed
the false promise that eating the forbidden fruit would
make them much different, much better, much more powerful and in control of things than they were. It was an
empty fantasy, and they found out very quickly that it
didn't work. Suddenly they realized that they were naked—

that they had nothing extra, nothing that made them more successful, more fulfilled, more anything. They were just themselves.

Compulsive and addicted people sometimes realize the same thing but only after a long time—and after much of their lives and many opportunities for real achievement have been sucked down the drain. It doesn't matter a whole lot what the addiction was—alcohol, mindless entertainment, cyberspace, or anything else.

Even before actual addiction sets in, the Internet can eat up time that really needs to be spent elsewhere. This happens when an Internet "gotta" replaces a *real* "gotta."

If someone's first thought upon awakening, or immediately after school or work is *I gotta check my e-mail*, that's not a good sign. Unless it's a professional or business obligation, e-mail is a convenience and a recreation, not a "gotta." Instant messaging is fun, just like the telephone—only glitzier—and communicating with friends is an important part of developing as a person. But when e-mailing friends and even people you've never met in person becomes an everyday "gotta," it's in control of your life.

Nowhere is being controlled truer than in the addicted world of cyberspace pornography. Visiting porn sites is *deadly*. There's no other word for it.

But it seldom seems that way at the start. The first time can even be unintentional. The pictures may at first be shocking, especially to a young viewer. They may even appear sick. But for many people, they do their job all too well. They jolt the sexual-response system into motion, and that's a very powerful thing. It's not always easy to keep it under control in normal circumstances. An additional, high-powered stimulus makes it even more difficult.

Addiction to Internet porn works just like addiction to other kinds of pornography, but much faster. It's available and often free any time someone logs on. Sometimes it's waiting in the form of spam.

That makes it easy. There's no going out to buy it secretly and then hiding it where others can't find it. It's easily gotten rid of. Even if pop-up windows lock you into a porn site, a flip of the power switch turns the screen blank and the filth is gone as though it had never been there.

But it's gone only from the screen. The images linger in the mind, and escalation often takes place. Escalation means seeking out the stuff increasingly often and needing stronger ("sicker") images to produce the desired interest and sexual response.

It's not true that porn affects and changes only people who are already sex-obsessed and "sick." That would be like saying alcohol affects only people who are already alcoholics. Porn can suck in and trap perfectly normal, good people. That's how people *become* sex-obsessed and sick. Eventually, a normal, good, romantic relationship seems boring, or merely a steppingstone to a possible super-charged sexual payoff.

Being controlled is never easy to face or admit. We don't like to admit that we are not in control. Sure, once in a while we get into a self-pitying mood and write—or at least think—second-rate poetry about being a victim. ("My life is a sadly ragged, tattered rope that fate has twisted and knotted until it is too weak and limp to be itself.") But for the most part, we want to feel in charge—even when we're not.

Admitting that something we chose has taken over too much of our life, or is coming close to doing so, is the first step toward regaining control. We can't get to the second, third, or any other step without the first. As Jesus said, only the truth will set us free (see John 8:32).

Words From the Word

The simple believe everything, but the clever consider their steps.

Proverbs 14:15

Other Voices

We should enter this increasingly sophisticated communications network with realism and confidence. If it is used competently and responsibly, it could offer an opportunity for spreading the evangelical word.

Pope John Paul II

Often people joke about being addicted to the Net, but...there are people out there who are essentially slaves to their computers.

Richard A. Davis, Internet Behavior Consultant

The first step is self-awareness. If we deny the possibility of any sort of Internet dependency or compulsive use of the Internet, then we're in trouble.

Andrew Careaga

Bottom Line

The Internet is a valuable—these days, almost necessary—tool. But precisely because it offers so many dazzling possibilities, it can easily be addictive, and users must look at their Net use with great honesty.

SEVEN

WATCH YOUR TONGUE AND SAVE A FOREST

I lie down among lions that greedily devour human prey; their teeth are spars and arrows, their tongues sharp swords.

Psalm 57:4

᪥

everal years ago, I almost set our church on fire. A gloriously burning golden calf got somewhat—actually, a *lot*—out of control in the sanctuary. Public thanks should go to Rob Brooks who was serving Mass and brought the fire under control at considerable risk to his hands. Ever since then, whenever I planned a liturgy, people would ask, "You're not using fire, are you?"

Fire is wonderful when it's controlled. When it's not, it brings pain, destruction, and disaster. Easy enough to understand, and usually we take care to keep genuine flames under control.

We're not always so careful with other kinds of fire—especially the kind in our mouth.

"Consider how small a fire can set a huge forest ablaze.

And the tongue is a fire" (James 3:5–6). We don't know what prompted James to make that comment, but he knew what he was talking about. The fire of gossip in particular can cause the beautiful forest of someone's life to be destroyed even before it has a chance to grow. Here's an example.

It's early March. Jenny is a high school junior. She's thinking of running for student government in May when officers are elected for the following school year.

On Friday night she goes out with David. He has a reputation for being a user, but Jenny doesn't believe it. She soon discovers there's a good reason for David's reputation. But she's strong, she delivers a strong "NO" right in his face, and she doesn't date him again. That part of her story is over.

She runs for student government and gets elected. Her senior year is a flurry of activity. She helps coordinate recycling efforts; heads a fund drive for expanding the computer lab; participates in a mentoring program; and establishes herself as a liaison to the City Council.

She doesn't do all this to get noticed and rewarded, but it happens anyway—with a scholarship to an excellent university. Because of her experience in student government, she majors in political science.

Jenny's college years are challenging and successful. Her senior high school year experience prompts her to get involved in similar activities on a college level. She graduates with honors and undertakes a two-year master's degree program. There she meets Brian, and they fall in love.

Jenny receives her master's degree, and she's ready to bring exciting ideas to a career in government. She and Brian are also making wedding plans.

A very nice forest—and in many ways just getting started.

But let's rewind to that March weekend eight years ago. Same date; again, she says no to David's pressure.

But this time there's a classmate, Sarah, who doesn't like Jenny. Jenny's date with David, given his reputation, provides Sarah with an opportunity.

Sarah spreads the story that quite a bit happened on that date. To feel okay about this, Sarah tells herself that it's *probably* true because…well, she heard some things about other girls that David took out.

When Jenny is unexpectedly sick for a few days, the explanation among the gossip crowd is that she's pregnant. When this gets back to Jenny, she's shattered. Some people who are repeating "Jenny and David" stories are her friends—or so she thought. "I heard she had an abortion" stories are starting, followed by "I heard it's her second one" stories.

It's enough to make her almost never want to be in public at school, no matter how false and slanderous the stories are. Of course, she *has* to attend school.

But she doesn't have to run for student government. And she decides not to. She's afraid that putting her name and face in front of the school right now in an election campaign will simply provoke more malicious stories.

The rest of the story plays out like dominos falling in reverse. Because she doesn't run for office, she doesn't spend her senior year in student government. She doesn't get the scholarship, she doesn't go to that particular university, she doesn't end up with degrees in political science, and she doesn't meet Brian.

The fire of gossip destroyed the forest that could have been and should have been, even before it had a chance to grow.

Yes, it's a fictional example. But impossible? Improbable? Too big a stretch of the imagination? No.

How many real possibilities for good things in real lives have been wiped out by gossip? It's a really unpleasant thought.

The kind of gossip we're talking about here isn't stuff like, "Emily *says* she's not interested in Joe, but I think she'd faint from joy if he asked her out." It's impossible to live on earth and never make a reference to anything going on in another person's life. But a remark like that does no harm, which is about the same as saying it's not sinful. That's the key—not sinful.

Now, believe me, I don't want to return to the days when being a person of faith meant studying a small encyclopedia of possible sins and worrying yourself silly over them. ("Have I committed *presumption?* Uh-oh...I think maybe I did last Wednesday. And that's a biggie because it's here in capital letters, bold print, and italics! Damn, my chances of going to hell just increased by 500 percent. *Oh no*—I just cussed, so I'm probably up to 650 percent!")

But there *are* a few words that we ought to refresh ourselves on. They describe wrong things that we may not fully realize are really sinful. If we have no desire to avoid sinful things, we can hardly call ourselves Catholic Christians. Here they are: *rash judgment, detraction,* and *calumny.* They're all sins against respect for the reputation of other people; you can find them in the *Catechism of the Catholic Church*, #2477.

Rash judgment is assuming without evidence that somebody did something wrong, or is an immoral person in general. This is pretty easy to do if a lot of other people are making the same assumption and saying so. It's easy to figure they must have some reason for saying those things, so what they're saying must be true.

What if "the reason for saying those things" is simply that they heard them, without any evidence, from other people? What if *the only "reason"* is "They say that..." and "I heard that..."?

Detraction is telling people about something wrong that another person really did, or about a fault that he or she really has, without any good reason for doing so.

To use an example from a previous chapter, if you know (from having seen it) that someone nearly always drinks himself into a pleasant buzz at baseball games, and you also know that this person has been unexpectedly asked to drive a vanload of kids home from the game, that's a reason for disclosing the information quietly to somebody who can make different arrangements. That's not detraction. Simply blabbing to everyone that this person drinks too much *is*.

Calumny (also known as *slander*) is literally making up—or repeating probably made up—stories about someone that could harm that person's reputation. This is just plain evil. Yet this is the category that includes most of the stories which attack someone's reputation sexually.

Imagine yourself as a heart surgeon. You are literally holding someone's heart in your hand. Obviously you have the power of life or death here. If you deliberately crushed that person's heart in your hand just because you didn't like him or her, you'd be a genuine monster.

But something very similar is at work when people gossip. Instead of the person's actual heart, the person's reputation is at stake, and the instrument of life or death is the tongue.

A person's reputation is sacred. We need to respect sacred things. To stain or ruin someone's reputation is like taking life from him or her. It's simply evil.

If you find yourself taking part in gossip more often than you should or taking part in gossip that should never be taking place, here are some ways to get out of the habit.

- *Find other ways of feeling okay.* People gossip for many reasons, but probably the most common one is that it gives a feeling of power and/ or being okay (usually as distinct from the person being gossiped about, who for some reason is not okay). Possessing information to be passed along seems to give status.
- There's nothing wrong with wanting to feel in control of life or wanting to have a respectable

status in a group. But gossiping about others is a cheap way to get those feelings; they don't last long either because they don't actually improve the gossiper as a person. That's why he/she needs to find still another person or situation to gossip about, similar to the way an alcoholic needs to keep drinking in order to feel okay.

Look for other ways to feel good about you all by yourself, to feel worthwhile and in control because of what *you have actually done*, not because of what you can say about others.

• *Think about protecting yourself.* "A gossip reveals secrets; therefore do not associate with a babbler" (Proverbs 20:19). Once again, the Book of Proverbs comes through with an on-target insight into life in any century. You cannot be part of a gossip crowd and expect never to be the subject of gossip yourself when you're not there. This isn't the most spiritual reason to avoid gossip, but it's certainly valid. If your friends routinely enjoy talking about people who are not present, what reason do you have to think that you won't be gossiped about when *you're* not there?

• *Consider the "two weeks to go" scenario.* This is a great test for any unkind thing you're tempted to say, whether it's about someone or to them personally. Would you still say it if you knew that person had only to weeks to live? Or knew that the person's mother or father had just died? Or if that person's brother, sister, or best friend were about to die?

Not likely. You wouldn't want to cause still further pain in a situation like that. So why say it and cause pain now?

- *Put possible gossip through this three-way test.* If it flunks any part of it, you should probably keep silent or find a different way of saying it.

1. *Is it true?* If you don't know for sure that something about someone is true, you probably shouldn't say it. The exceptions involve trying to help someone. For example, if you hear that someone has been talking about suicide—that's worth reporting to a person who can take action. That's not just gossip for the sake of gossip.

2. *Is it necessary?* Even if you know that something is true, ask yourself if it's really necessary to repeat it. "Necessary" is a very important word in this case, and it's very precise. If you know about something that is likely to cause harm, and you can prevent the harm by speaking up, then it's necessary to say what you know. If not, keep the facts to yourself.

3. *Is it kind?* Let's say something about someone is true, and let's say there's a genuine, justifiable reason for telling someone else about it. Is the way you go about it kind, or is it more like an attack?

"For lack of wood, the fire goes out, and where there is no whisperer, quarreling ceases" (Proverbs 26:20). How many hurt feelings, broken friendships, bitter misunderstandings, and even violent confrontations could be avoided if there were no "whisperers"?

But people don't carry tales where there is no ear to listen to them. Quietly let it be known, as much by example as by statement, that you don't believe in or like harmful gossip. You don't have to appear obnoxiously righteous to do that. Still, it's a tough stand to make, and it takes a lot of believing in yourself in order to do it. But it might rub off. Maybe at least some of your friends will follow your example.

It could put out a lot of fires...and maybe save someone's forest.

Words From the Word

Death and life are in the power of the tongue.

Proverbs 18:21

Keep your tongue from evil, and your lips from speaking deceit.

Psalm 34:13

Other Voices

Whoever gossips to you will gossip about you.

Spanish proverb

They [gossipers] come together like the Coroner's Inquest, to sit upon the murdered reputations of the week.

William Congreve

Bottom Line

It's not always easy to sense where relatively harmless gossip stops being harmless and becomes the actual sins of rash judgment, detraction, and calumny. But if we intend to be Christians, we have to develop that sense.

EIGHT

BEFORE SOMEONE REALLY GETS HURT

Then Jesus said to him, "Put your sword back into its place; for all who take the sword will perish by the sword."

Matthew 26:52

❧

H ere's a Jack and Jill story, but it's not about going up and down hills, and the only pail of water possibly involved in the story would be a bucket of tears. Read all of it before you decide it's just too weird to spend time on.

The Story

Jack and Jill are on a date. They like each other. It's not serious yet, but they feel comfortable talking about plans for the future, including family and the kids they'll probably have.

"You want to have a son?" Jill asks.

"Sure," Jack answers. "And a daughter. Maybe a couple of each."

"What do you want your boy to be like?"

"Well, I want him to be strong and healthy, especially strong enough to fight. Tough. I want him to be able to hurt people."

"How much should he hurt people?" Jill continues.

"As much as he wants. That would be up to him. If he put somebody in the hospital for a while, I'd be proud."

"How would he do that?"

"Doesn't matter. I want him to know how to swing a baseball bat, but not for baseball, and he should handle knives the way most kids handle pencils. He should learn that stuff by maybe twelve or thirteen. Guns could wait until a little later, fourteen, fifteen maybe. And I want him to hang out with other guys doing the same thing."

"How do you expect him to stay out of trouble?"

"Well, he probably *wouldn't* stay out of trouble! So what? So he'd get suspended or expelled or sent to juvie or detention—it'd be worth it. Look at all the kicks he'd get out of being violent. I'd be proud of him and happy for him. And what about you, Jill—you want a daughter?"

"Sure," Jill answers, "and, you know, it's freaky because what you just said is pretty much how I want my daughter to be."

"Really?" Jack is intrigued and glad to know Jill is on the same wave length when it comes to dreams for their children, whether they have them together or not.

"Yeah. Well, I'm not sure about the knives and guns stuff. Beating people up, maybe. But at least I want her hanging around guys who do that stuff. A gang, probably. Even if they aren't in a gang, I want my daughter to think that violent guys are cool, and hang around with them, starting in her early teens anyway."

"What do you hope would happen?"

"Well," Jill answers, "her schoolwork would be shot when she starts doing that because good grades don't exactly go along with that kind of lifestyle."

"Really."

"She might have to go to summer school or repeat a year. She might even drop out, or get kicked out. That would be cool."

"I know. You'd be so proud of her, Jill. What else?"

"Well, the guys she'd hang out with would see girls as toys, you know what I mean? They'd be really good at talking sweet to a girl—it makes the girl think there's a wonderful, soft side to this dangerous, violent guy. That's a real turn-on for some girls. You know how some girls go around saying, 'But he can be so sweet and gentle when he wants to.' It's all a game and a lie, of course."

"And then what?"

"Well, she'll get talked into being used."

"You mean, like...raped?"

"Well," Jill says thoughtfully, "I don't think I'd want my daughter exactly *raped*. But she'd put out, be available for a guy who hurts people and breaks things but talks sweet. And she'd think it's because he loves her."

"You want her to get pregnant?"

"That'd be cool. You know—fifteen, sixteen and pregnant by this gang stud...her school all messed up...maybe a drug problem that could affect the baby along with all the other stuff...yeah, that'd be really cool."

The End

We'll stop there before you puke.

Jack and Jill are fictional characters. But if they were real...if two actual teens had the above conversation *and meant it,* how would you describe them and their plans?

For starters, let's try ugly, mean, vicious, monstrous, sadistic, depraved, hateful, evil, and incredibly perverted. It's so evil and perverted that you can't imagine two young people wanting that lifestyle for their future children.

So why do many young people choose that exact lifestyle for themselves?

Again, the above conversation sounds so sickly impossible because we cannot imagine anyone wanting those things for their children. So why do some young people even toy with the possibility of those things for themselves?

People give various explanations.

"Their families don't go to church; they don't even pray." "They live in a bad neighborhood." "Their families don't have enough money." "They give in to peer pressure because they're low on self-esteem." "They're bored and looking for some excitement." "They're already misfits, so they get together with other misfits and form a gang." "Their families don't know how to affirm and support one another." "They're rebelling like any other young people, they're just carrying it too far."

Maybe there's some truth in all those explanations, depending on the situation. But any person who is into violence, or dancing around the edge of it, is looking for something he or she needs in a place where he or she will never find it—at least not without paying an often heavy price. And perhaps one of the things they're looking for is glamour.

"It's all about image," a young man wrote me from prison a few weeks ago, where he is serving time for a life of addiction and violence that began when he was in his early teens. "A lot of the music promotes it. It gives you the image of a punk, gangster, freak, and somehow that looks cool. And I've watched every mafia and gang-type movie available. Even though they all have a common denominator of death or incarceration, they still glorify the life of a violent person for all but ten minutes. I was the type that sees the 'glory,' and said, 'But I won't get caught.' I see the Godfather's daughter die, but tune it out. All I see is the Rolls Royce, the family parties, the 'glory.' The beginnings are filled with beating people up, getting mass girls, the clothes and the jewelry, and it all looks cool, but it doesn't end that way."

If a friend is on the verge of a violent lifestyle, here are three signs you might recognize. You're the one who will see the signs first in classmates and friends, which means you're the one who can try to do something about it before it leads to life-changing actions.

It's harder to see the same signs in yourself, just as it's difficult to see the parade when you're marching in it. But, as with a real parade, it's possible to step outside it for a few minutes and take a look. If you need to do that, do it.

1. *Today is all that counts.* This means tuning out everything beyond the current moment, including the consequences of risky behavior. Have fun, feel cool today. Tomorrow? Tomorrow may not come and in any case it isn't here yet, so why even think about it? It can start in areas that aren't violent, like grades. Some people can be carrying a 57 percent average in three classes, but as long as there are five or six days left in the quarter, they have this brain-dead idea that things will somehow get better…so why not have some fun today?

2. *No big deal; I'm good; everything's cool [no matter what].* "So I got kicked off the bus for fighting. So I got suspended for beating up somebody. So I have to go to this stupid juvie court hearing and maybe get put on house arrest. It's no big deal. Two of my friends are the same way, and everything's cool with them. We'll be okay. So I don't always keep all the rules— it's not like I'm going to rob a bank or something."

   Remaining hopeful even when things are going wrong is good. Pretending that a bad situation doesn't matter and may as well not exist—that's not good. That's denial.

3. *It doesn't matter; nothing really matters.* "I don't care"

is one thing when it's a response to a Friday after-
noon detention. When it's a response to the possibility of being suspended or expelled, failing an entire
year, going to juvenile court, having a police record,
being put on house arrest, getting sent to a correc-
tional institution, or causing your family to be sued...
that's dangerous. It's true that "I don't care" is sometimes a defense mechanism, a way of trying to tune
out the pain of something. But an inner buildup of
anger and hopelessness can lead someone to say, "I
don't care" about anything and everything and mean
it. A person who literally doesn't care what happens
to himself or herself is dangerous both to self and to
others. The prospect of consequences for his or her
actions, even grim consequences, is no longer a re-
straint on behavior.

Can you stop a friend's downhill slide into a lifestyle
of violence? I'm certainly not going to say, "Sure, and
here's the guaranteed formula for doing it." Trying to
change things is going to be a little risky and there are
no guarantees for success. You'll have to stick your neck
out. How much do you want to give it a shot? It helps a
lot of you to have company, meaning others who also
want to keep that friend from digging a hole that will
eventually trap him or her.

If nothing else, here's something you *don't* do: Don't
be amused—not even a little—by what that person is
beginning to do. I've taught more than one kid who got
into trouble through violent behavior of one kind or

another. In many cases there were friends who could see it coming, sometimes actually saw it happening, but often laughed or grinned a little and said, "You're crazy, man."

Reactions and statements like that will be taken as *compliments,* as affirmations, signs of success, signs of being somebody.

I often wonder what might have happened if any of those kids had been confronted by a group of friends (the larger the better) who had the guts to say, "We care about you and because we do, we're worried about you. We hope you change for *your* sake and get out of what you're getting into." At least some of the outcomes might have been different.

It's a hard message to give somebody, and, as I said, it helps if you have company when you say it. "Peer pressure" has a bad ring to it, but peers don't have to be the bad guys, the ones who lure somebody into trouble, whether it's violence or something else. Peers can be the good guys, the ones who work together to save someone *from* trouble.

Too often, they don't realize that they have power for good. They don't band together and work at it—or they take the first negative response ("Get off my back—I know what I'm doing") as final and stop trying.

Remember the question Jill asked Jack—what do you want for your kids? That's one way to get a friend to begin to think about the consequences of his or her actions. What kind of dad or mom do you want to be for your kids? What kind *are* you going to be if you keep doing what you're doing? Do your kids deserve that—don't they deserve better?

Almost everyone cares about the kids he or she has or will have. Even teens who don't seem to care about their grades or the next several months or years of their own future might be startled into awareness when they make a connection between their current behavior and their future kids.

The kind of person they're becoming is exactly the kind of parent and role model their kids are going to be stuck with.

Ask them if they want that.

Words From the Word

Depart from evil, and do good; seek peace, and pursue it.

Psalm 34:14

And the peace of God, which surpasses all understanding, will guard your hearts and your minds in Christ Jesus.

Philippians 4:7

Other Voices

Violence is the last refuge of the incompetent.

Isaac Asimov

Profile of a thug is the worse like a curse / You doomed you done, room enough for one.

Christian rapper BB Jay

Deeds of violence in our society are performed largely by those trying to establish their self-esteem, to defend their self-image, and to demonstrate that they, too, are significant.

Rollo May

Bottom Line

A violent lifestyle can seem glamorous—but it's a loser...along with being just plain extremely *wrong*. If someone you know is getting sucked into it, care enough about them to attempt to stop it.

NINE

CLIQUES: A NASTY SEVEN-LETTER WORD

Have you not made distinctions among yourselves
and become judges with evil thoughts?

James 2:4

〰️

Clique—there's just nothing nice about the word. It
doesn't even sound nice. It stirs up negative feelings
no matter who or where you are.

People who belong to a group that's called a clique
resent the label. People who are targeted by a clique resent the ill treatment. People who *wish* they belonged to
one resent being excluded. People who don't belong and
don't want to belong resent the negative social waves
that a clique makes.

Cliques are too often an unpleasant fact of life. Like
"peer pressure," the word *clique* suggests adolescent life,
but that's not completely true. There are cliques in of-
fices, professional sports teams, university faculties…
almost anywhere.

Webster defines the word as "a small, highly exclusive

circle of people." I've heard other, informal definitions that we can't print here, mainly from people outside a clique who were being put down by the people inside it.

A group of close friends (which is a very good thing) and a clique (which is not) may appear similar in some ways. Sometimes a group is unfairly labeled a clique. Five to fifteen people who genuinely enjoy one another's company, and who therefore usually prefer to be with one another, do not constitute a clique.

Add the following characteristics, however, and it becomes clear what makes a clique different from the above.

1. *Total exclusiveness.* "People who do not have our approval (because they're not like us) cannot enter our circle, get invited to our parties, or sit at the same lunch table—unless we're celebrating 'Be Nice to Nerds and Geeks Week.'"
2. *Superiority and snobbishness.* "We're...well, better, definitely much cooler, than others. We know what life is *really* all about."
3. *(Not always, but frequently) Harassment.* "Uncool people deserve to be put down for being stupid, and we have a lot of fun giving them what they deserve."

Crazily, these same people may also talk about being Christian, loving others, and reaching out to those less fortunate. Apparently, this does not include those who are less fortunate when it comes to social coolness ratings.

Cliques are nothing new; they existed even among

early Christian believers, including those who were old enough to know better. Paul addressed the problem in the very first chapter of his First Letter to the Corinthians. Some of them were forming exclusive, cliquish groups based on who had taught them, or whom they followed as a Christian leader.

> For it has been reported to me about you, my brothers...that there are rivalries among you. I mean that each of you is saying, "I belong to Paul," or "I belong to Apollos," or "I belong to Cephas" [Peter], or "I belong to Christ." Is Christ divided? (1 Cor 1:11–13).

It sounds as though there were three competing cool groups of Corinthian Christians centered around Paul, Apollos, and Peter (none of whom started or wanted this). Those on the outside, low on the social ladder, were saying, "*They* may not think we're cool, but *Jesus* knows we're okay, and they're going to learn a hard lesson when Jesus comes again! *Then* we'll find out who the real Christians are and who aren't!"

Sound familiar?

Maybe you'll make it through all your schools, all your workplaces, and even activities at the Senior Citizen Center without ever encountering a clique. And maybe you'll win every lottery and be appointed Magistrate of Planet Earth, too. They're equally likely.

If you're like most people, both growing and grown, you'll have to deal with a clique situation from some vantage point, and it's one of the tougher things life throws you. We'll look at four clique-oriented situations and list some things to think about for each one.

1. *You—and perhaps your friends—are the target of a clique.* This group enjoys putting you down, letting you know where you stand on the social ladder (at the bottom), and trying to make you feel inferior and even miserable. You're excluded from parties, hear whispered comments in the hall or laughter behind your back, and when you approach *the* group the circle turns inward giving you an excellent view of everyone's shoulder blades. Perhaps you even find nasty notes in your desk.

   Here are a few things you can do—and not do. First the nots.

   Don't let them *actually make you feel inadequate or not worthwhile.* True, you know deep inside that you're not a glob of worthless scum. Nevertheless, it's easy to let their opinions and actions dull the shine of your self-image.

   Don't let it do that. It's one thing to feel hurt. (That, believe it or not, is temporary.) It's another to feel defective. Don't. Some of the world's most successful people, including some movie stars, were *way* out of the cool group during their school years.

   Don't let negative feelings like resentment consume and control you. When that happens, your performance in school and other activities declines, and you spend a lot of time on empty fantasizing about turning the tables or even getting revenge. That's letting them take over in areas of your life that they really cannot control unless you let them. And actually plotting and trying to take revenge...we've had one tragic instance after another in recent years of what a loser and a failure that is.

One of the best responses to hurtful snobbery is called *"cordial, confident, confrontation."* "Cordial" because you behave genuinely pleasantly. "Confident" because you don't hang your head and act defeated. "Confrontation" because you don't slink away and try to pretend you don't care.

Example: You hear a name or a comment tossed your way. Put a smile on your face (yes, a *smile*), keep your head up, and say (*pleasantly and confidently*), "You know, if that was intended to hurt, it worked. But if you expect me to believe it, forget it. I don't. Have a nice day."

2. *You're not the target of a clique, and you don't belong to it either—but you wish you belonged.* Are you sure? Being accepted by the people who seem to run the social scene may seem like a big promotion, a boost to your self-image. But what price will you have to pay? What kind of unwritten rules will you have to follow?

Will you have to act and talk as though all adults are idiotic fools, even though you know better? Will you occasionally have to raise some hell, break some rules, let your grades slip, buy different clothes, listen to music you don't really care for, sneak a little alcohol or weed, hide your faith—or let go of it altogether? "I can't get into the cool group," a student complained to me one day several years ago. That group was into some, let's say, negative stuff; it wasn't any big mystery. "Good," I answered. "There's much less chance of your life getting royally screwed up."

Ask yourself what holds this group together. Is it genuine friendship, a shared interest in good things? Or are they held together mainly by feeling that they're better than others, or by activities that cross the line of the law or common sense? Is the group a collection of different personalities who learn from one another's differences, or is there a dull sameness about them underneath their glitzy lifestyle?

If you find yourself wanting to wear a glitzy piece of clothing, you check the price first. You think about what you're going to have to give up to have it. It's the same with wanting to fit in with any social group. Check the price first.

3. *You feel torn between two groups.* You've gained acceptance into a popular group. Maybe you're not certain that it's really a snobby clique, but the people seem more exciting, more interesting, maybe even more with it than some of your old friends do. You don't want to abandon your old friends, but you don't want to miss a chance to make new friends, either.

Consider whether it's really an either/or decision. Maybe it is—meaning that at some later point you're actually told, or at least you get the very definite feeling, that hanging around your old friends is going to threaten your new "membership." Or perhaps you're "allowed" to hang around them only when your new friends aren't doing anything.

In that case, it's pretty obvious that being included comes with a price. It's called being owned, being told how to behave—in this case somewhat like a traitor. Then you really do have a decision to make, and it involves what kind of person you want to be.

But it might seem to be an either/or situation only because *you* think it is and make it that way. If your new friends are not a hard-core clique, they'll leave you free to associate with your old friends when you want to. And if your old ones are true friends, they'll leave you free to branch out. Maybe the two groups will never completely come together and you may have to balance yourself sort of delicately between them— but that can actually be kind of fun. And it means that you're in control of your life and your relationships.

4. *If you're completely honest, you have to admit that you belong to a clique.* This might be the toughest of all the situations because it's an awfully difficult admission to make. For a long time, you might have told yourself, "It's not a sin to be popular! Why hang around people with different interests, especially if those interests are...kind of dumb." But deep inside you know that's a cover-up. You know that when people consider your group snobby, and sometimes downright mean, they're right in many cases.

You have to ask yourself some tough questions. If

the group is hurting others with gossip and put-downs, *do you really want to continue to be associated with it?* If our faith is going to be anything more than a thin, cheap, stick-on label, it makes some demands. One of the central, absolute core demands is not deliberately hurting others.

If popularity and image are the only, or at least principal, things holding the group together, you have to decide whether that's all you want out of your personal relationships. Lasting friendships are built on more than coolness ratings.

The status and the ratings disappear and the groups dissolve anyway, as people move from one arena to another—grade school to high school, high school to college, college to adult life. Yes, you want to succeed socially at each level. But you don't want to sell out your integrity for a temporary success.

Consider that you may have more influence on your group than you think. Maybe you can change things—persuade others to stop the meanness, dump the snobbishness, and even try to become more inclusive.

It's not likely to happen overnight. You will have to confront your friends openly. You will almost certainly deal with resistance. You will almost certainly be asked why you're changing from cool to uncool (as others see it). Tell them that you're not. Being a Christian *is* cool. Even if you don't use those words, you need to believe it in your heart and gut.

It's definitely a risk. It will take skill, perseverance,

and a ton of Christian guts. But it just might succeed. Pray for the skill, the perseverance, and the ton of Christian risk-taking guts.

The key to surviving a clique situation, whether from the inside or the outside, is to do what God does. God believes in you, the real you. Do that yourself. Believe in—and be and be proud of—the real you. Don't let clique pressure lead you to be somebody else.

Words From the Word

For who sees anything different in you? What do you have that you did not receive? And if you received it, why do you boast as if it were not a gift?

1 Corinthians 4:7

Let us not compete against one another, envying one another.

Galatians 5:26

Other Voices

Every clique is a refuge for incompetence. Its instincts and actions are those of the pack.

Madame Chiang Kai-shek

Snobbery is the pride of those not sure of their own position.

Minnesota proverb

No one can make you feel inferior without your permission.

Eleanor Roosevelt

Bottom Line

Cliques happen. Maybe you're in one, maybe you're way out of one, maybe it just doesn't matter to you, but you dislike the idea. In any of those situations, what do you think Jesus would do in your place?

CHAPTER TEN

DATING AND LOVE: A MICRO-GUIDE (AND, BY THE WAY, HOW FAR IS TOO FAR?)

So Jacob served seven years for Rachel, and they seemed to him but a few days because of the love he had for her.

Genesis 29:20

❧

Dating (dāt′ing) n. [ME. *dætnig* < OE. *dœtig* to eat pizza together with an opposite gender life form] 1. a custom common among the young in which a guy and a girl meet at certain intervals to compare and review notes from World Cultures and other classes 2. a process through which young men learn, from a refining feminine influence, that it is not cool to burp in a restaurant 3. a process of premarital, intergender socialization invented by God as a preparation for the sacrament of matrimony.

Let's go with the third definition.

Long, long ago, in a garden far, far away, God introduced this guy named Adam to this girl named Eve and said, "I think you two should consider going together. If it works out, we can move to some further possibilities."

On the first date, Adam said, "Let me show you the animals I've named!" As it turned out, Eve loved animals—although she had a strange, uneasy feeling about the snake—and she and Adam were quickly tight. In fact, on the third date, Adam said, "Eve, I've never felt this way about any girl before." Soon—to use a phrase from the era that produced Elvis and a generation of teenagers who are now kind of old—they were "going steady." And God looked down from heaven and said, "Cool— My will is being done."

Okay, so it was a blind date, and they didn't have a lot of other choices. And, okay, so God didn't exactly say exactly that. But the point is this: *God* invented and personally blessed this guy/girl relationship exploring-and-building thing.

So, God has a serious concern that it goes right. That's why, when Jack asks Jill to go with him and Jill says yes, and they begin to spend evenings together, God probably feels the same thing Jack's parents and Jill's parents feel: a combination of *pride* and *worry*.

Pride because in general things are going the way they're supposed to; their kids are growing up, and that's supposed to happen. You don't have kids so you can preserve them in bottles at a cute, young age. You have great dreams for their happiness, which for most people involves finding one special person to love who will love them in return.

And *worry* because the dating relationship could take a really wrong, life-changing turn; or it could, in the end, cause more pain than it did happiness. Anyone who doesn't see that hasn't been looking at reality lately. The dating scene is not always a safe place, physically and emotionally.

Obviously, that shouldn't be the main focus in thinking about dating. ("WARNING: You have a date this weekend! WARNING! DANGER!") But a total "nothing could ever go wrong" attitude makes as much sense as not taking a jacket on a trip to the Arctic.

First of all, let's remember that you don't have to be a constant part of the dating scene. It's not the same as if you don't breathe, you don't live. If you don't date at this point in your life, you don't date, that's all. Not going with anyone in particular is a perfectly normal teen and young adult lifestyle.

But I've known young people who nearly panicked if they were between relationships for more than a couple weeks. It's as though they had to be *going with* someone in order to *be* someone. That's self-insulting, as though all your worth comes from being connected to someone else.

You also don't have to live up to some kind of Perfect Date image in order to have fun dating. I'm not recommending being a dull slob or not putting some effort into making dates interesting and fun. (It's possible to slip into the get-a-pizza-and-watch-a-DVD rut, for example.

It's difficult for the interesting qualities about you and your date to sparkle while you're both watching action adventure heroes blow up buildings and make cars leap from one side of the Grand Canyon to the other.)

You're not born with a complete set of dating and relationship-building skills either, and having to learn them is okay, and it's okay to learn them at different ages. A few days ago a former student, now a high school senior, called with a problem: how to ask this particular girl out (even though they're in class together and sometimes eat lunch together).

"There's a secret method," I told him.

"What is it?"

"*You ask her.*"

"That's scary," he said.

"Did I say it wasn't?"

Okay, so Jack asks Jill to go out with him, Jill says yes, and they begin spending evenings and weekends together and find themselves becoming close. Is this love? Sure could be. It might be more accurate to say it sure could *become* love. *Love* is a small word with an extremely broad range. Let's use an example from another area.

Picture a baseball field with a bunch of six-year-olds. An adult is gently tossing the ball at the batter, trying to make it easy to hit. Once in a while, that actually happens. When it does, some other kids scramble around and shout at one another…and often the ball just rolls and rolls. Is this baseball? Sure. It's baseball with the players' skills in the very beginning, somewhat clumsy stages. Does that make it stupid? Of course not. It's not only not stupid, it's necessary. Nobody begins playing baseball with nearly professional skills.

Now let's move these kids up to age twelve or so. Now they hit the ball a lot more often and catch it a lot more often. Is this baseball? Of course, and at a considerably higher level than the first. Still, it's a long way from professional baseball.

We could cite many more levels of baseball, but you get the point. A person's ability to play grows, sharpens, and deepens. It's all baseball—*along a broad range of ability.* Getting better *usually* goes along with getting older, but it's not automatic. Someone who spends little effort at growing might get older but not necessarily better; he or she might still play on a relative beginner's level even at age twenty-five or thirty.

Love—being able to love—is similar in many ways.

Are Jack and Jill in love? Sure. How deep a level of love? To them, it may feel like this is it, this is my life, my future, my destiny, this is what and who I was born for. To other people, it's difficult to judge. The point is, let's hope Jack and Jill make a good judgment (that's very different than having a deep feeling) about how mature their love is and how lasting it is likely to become.

Because when you're in love, you want to celebrate it. If two people in love don't do anything to celebrate the relationship, they've got the ink from grammar review sheets going through their circulatory systems instead of blood.

The big question is...*how* to celebrate.

If you listen to the culture around us, you'll find a simple, easy answer: have sex. Get busy. Do it. The terms get increasingly cruder, and the words themselves practically shout that they have nothing at all to do with romance, caring, or love.

Back to our baseball example. Take a couple of, let's say, sixteen-year-old players who really love the game and are very serious about it. Now—because of that—put them on a major league field with major league responsibilities…and expect them to handle it all. What's going to happen?

It'll be exciting for a brief period. But it will almost certainly set their baseball development *back* rather than forward. They're not meant to handle it at this level yet.

Celebrating an initial level of love by having sex—no matter how genuine that initial level may be—is like that. Sex is not small stuff; sex is meant to be major league love.

The solution, obviously, is not to stay at least five feet away from each other and toss love notes written in the inside of burger wrappers. The relationship needs some touch. Determining what kind and how much leads us to the classic dating question: "How far is too far?"

It's a very honest question for any dating couple who genuinely want to express affection and love, yet keep away from any possibility of just using each other, and avoid paying a price later for what felt like a good idea at the time.

So here's a list and a scale of increasingly intense ways in which human beings can physically express affection and love. There's nothing on it that you don't know about.

1. Holding hands. 2. Hugging. 3. Light kiss on the cheek. (So far, these are all nonsexual gestures.) 4. Close cuddling and snuggling. 5. Light kiss on the lips. 6. Prolonged, deep, wet kiss. 7. Hands exploring above the waist. 8. Hands exploring below the waist. 9. Intercourse or oral sex. (There's a belief among many young people that oral sex "isn't really sex." That's like saying bringing food to your mouth with a gravy ladle, instead of the usual fork or spoon, isn't really eating. Of *course* it's sex! What else would it be?)

Ironically, the numbering makes it sound like a game, a list of mechanical techniques—in other words, like using someone. But that's precisely what the list is intended to help avoid.

Okay, we can giggle about the list, and Older Folke can frown, growl, and pretend to be outraged, but the list is very practical. *How far is too far?*

Teens who participate in programs such as PSI (Postponing Sexual Involvement) where the scale originated say that 5.5 is the limit: a really romantic kiss. After that, the rush of hormones can easily take over and pull the couple into things that were not planned and are often regretted.

Some people may think, *"5.5 is all I get?"* Notice that the love content there is zero. The focus is not on caring; it's on payoff.

And it reminds us of still another baseball reference. Degrees of physical exploring are commonly referred to as getting to first base, second base, and so forth. In spite of being coarse and selfish, there is something crudely honest about those terms. They describe a *playground* where somebody has a good time and then leaves—and possibly brags about what he or she accomplished while there.

Ask yourself a blunt question: Is that what you want your body to be—somebody's playground? Your body is more precious than that. You're worth more than that.

A final observation: *Males and females are not alike!* Yes, friends, it's true. We don't look alike, think alike, act alike, feel alike, tinkle alike, and sexually we don't *react* alike. A guy's sexual fire ignites a lot faster. A couple can be cuddling and kissing and the girl is floating on clouds of romance and a wonderful, tingling feeling of being cherished and chosen—while the guy is absolutely on fire.

There's no fault here; it just is. A guy reaches his sexual peak, in terms of sexual response, at around seventeen or eighteen. That didn't used to be a problem because many marriages began at around that age or only slightly later. That was before high school, before college, before all the career preparation that modern society has made necessary. Our bodies haven't adjusted to this era of delayed marriage, and it doesn't look like they're going to. Puberty, in fact, starts on the average three to four years earlier than it did a little over a hundred years ago.

A guy on fire needs to switch from masculine hormones (which every guy has) to manly guts (which a lot of guys *don't* have) and say something like, "This is really getting to me. We need to back off so I can cool off, because I don't want something to happen that shouldn't happen."

He needs to know that this does not mean he's less than a real man. It's the exact opposite.

His girlfriend needs to know it too, and to know that it does not mean she isn't attractive, desirable, and positively sexy. It's the exact opposite.

Why so much concentration on what *not* to do? Because dating is a lot more fun when there's no pressure, no using, and no regrets.

Why date at all? Let's go back to our original whimsical example. God looks down at Adam and Eve and says, "Cool—My will is being done."

That's one reason. Okay, it's not first on your list of Reasons Why I Want to Spend Time With a Certain Cute Person. ("Want to go out? We'll be fulfilling God's will, you know." With all due respect to God—and I'm sure God understands—that is *not* a good opening line.)

But the reason is real. In a good, respectful dating relationship (which God invented), God's will is being done in many, many ways. Two people are growing, learning, and discovering themselves and each other. It may lead to a marvelous ending that becomes a marvelous beginning called a wedding day. All of which God planned and wants.

When you're dating, there's three of you involved.

Words From the Word

Let me see your face, let me hear your voice; for your voice is sweet, and your face is lovely.

Song of Solomon 2:14

You have ravished my heart with a glance of your eyes.

Song of Solomon 3:9

Other Voices

Immature love says: "I love you because I need you." Mature love says, "I need you because I love you."

Erich Fromm

Intense love does not measure; it just gives.

Mother Teresa

The course of true love never did run smooth.

Shakespeare

I wanna be the one to make you happy / I wanna be the one to give you hope / But...we've got to take it slow / ...'Cause in these crazy times we're living / Love can turn into regret.

Celine Dion

Bottom Line

What we call "dating" was literally planned and blessed by God. Because we're imperfect, it sometimes leads to permanent joy, and it sometimes leads to painful fallout. When you're dating, you should hope for the former and avoid things that may lead to the latter.

ELEVEN

WHEN HEROES STUMBLE AND FALL

So David sent messengers to get her, and she came
to him, and he lay with her.

2 Samuel 11:4

❦

Students adored him...people gravitated toward him because he did a good job," the newspaper report said, quoting someone's description of a man who had been voted Teacher of the Year two years before at a high school in a large Midwestern city. He had been teaching in the school system for fourteen years. He was considered a hero, an inspiration, the kind of teacher you hope to get—and when you do, you remember him or her for years afterward as someone who made a difference in your life.

One year after being named Teacher of the Year, he pleaded guilty to several counts of sexual misconduct involving three of his students.

We like to put people in easy categories—good guys and bad guys, for example, even though we know that nearly everyone is a mix of good and not so good, and sometimes *very* not so good. So when a "good guy" who seems *especially good* does something that's *especially bad,* it sends our minds swirling into a "How can this be?" state.

It's called scandal—bad behavior by someone who was supposed to model good behavior; bad example from an expected role model. Sometimes it's major and becomes public, locally or even nationally. Sometimes the audience is much smaller, perhaps only you, as when you see someone whom you admire very drunk, or discover that he or she is having an affair.

Scandalous behavior by a hero isn't new. Three thousand years ago, King David committed adultery with Bathsheba, and then when she turned up pregnant, he arranged for her husband to be killed in battle so he could marry her.

A high-profile position doesn't make anyone immune to temptation or free from sin. Many political and religious leaders of all times and cultures have set a terrible example. A newspaper columnist gave one of our recent presidents "an A for political brilliance and an F for personal behavior."

Sometimes the more famous a person is, the less we are surprised by his or her behavior. No one is very shocked anymore when an NBA star admits or even brags about his sexual conquests. Few people gasp in shock when they learn that an entertainment idol has been living a drug-ridden lifestyle. Almost no one even raises an eyebrow upon learning that a rap star has been busted for a barroom brawl or illegal possession of a weapon. We figure that "it goes with the territory." This is both untrue and very unfair to the many political, sports, and entertainment figures who live positively virtuous lives.

When an admired person sets a very bad example, two things immediately come up for review. One is our opinion of the person. The other is our outlook on life, our own standards for behavior. At times like this, it's easy to make one or more of four very wrong conclusions.

1. *Probably almost everybody does it.* If a person with a long criminal record for robbery is arrested for passing bad checks, we don't gasp in shock and say, "Well, robbery, yes, but I never *dreamed* he would write a bad check!" We're not tempted to think that four out of five people are writing bad checks.

   But when an admired coach is found to be having an affair, it's tempting to think that many married people, maybe the majority, are unfaithful at one time or another. When an admired youth minister is arrested for DUI, it's easy to think that most adults abuse alcohol now and then. When the vice president of the student council turns up pregnant or loses a scholarship for handing in a downloaded research report, it's easy to think that practically all teens are having sex or cheating in school.

   It's just not so, and it's a mistake to think so. It's also extremely unfair because it puts good, honest, faithful, moral people into a "they just haven't been caught yet" category.

2. *If they can do it, then it (or something not so "big" in the same category) must not be so bad.* When people lower their standards of behavior, they seldom make a single, one-shot decision to do so. The lowering of ideals and standards usually starts small, and witnessing bad example can be a major factor in getting it started.

For example, people don't look in the mirror one morning and think, *You know, I'd probably be a really successful thief. I'm going to try it out.* But if the vice principal is caught diverting school funds into his or her bank account, it suddenly doesn't seem so terrible to dip a hand into the cafeteria money box while the lunch lady is distracted. ("What's taking a few bucks gonna hurt? The VP siphoned off four thousand dollars, and the school is still here.")

Few young people make a one-time decision to become obsessed with sex. But if the football coach is seen coming out of a strip bar or an adult video store, checking out an Internet porn site may start to seem pretty harmless. ("Everybody has a dark side they give in to now and then; it's just human nature.")

When an admired person sets a bad example, we have to remember that an action is what it is, regardless of who does it. If a Mafia crime boss steals fifty thousand dollars, that's theft. If the pope steals fifty thousand dollars, that's theft. (I'm certain the latter is a *very* low-percentage possibility.) And nobody's theft of fifty thousand dollars makes somebody else's theft of ten dollars okay.

3. *What they represent is probably corrupt too.* Politics and religion are easy targets, particularly when a political or religious leader does something very wrong. A nasty bit of corruption in City Hall hits the morning paper or the evening news, and people all over the city are saying, "Just goes to show you: government is crooked. It's all deals and payoffs. Everything is under the table and behind closed doors. You can't stop it."

So, they decide to ignore city politics and civic issues. They stay home on Election Day, grumbling that their vote can't change a hopeless state of affairs. They may pass on their prejudiced view of government to their children, who then decide that a class in civics or American government is about as useful as a class in underwater basket weaving. That's sad and wrong. Religion suffers when a leader does something wrong. You hear, "What a hypocrite! They stand up there on Sunday or sit there at their meetings and tell *us* how to behave, and then they go out and do the opposite. I swear, sometimes I think it's all phony." Notice that this seems to provide a wonderful excuse for abandoning religion or at least not taking it very seriously—how convenient.

If every single representative of a religion, an organization, or a businesses is proven guilty of immoral, deceitful behavior, we can rightfully conclude that what they represent is dishonest by its nature. But one, two, or even quite a few out of thousands of representatives—that's not enough to mentally convict the whole community and the ideas it stands for.

4. *I'll bet a lot of "them" are like that.* Stereotyping is never fair. It's particularly unjust when people are put under suspicion simply because they're similar in some ways to a person who has behaved wrongly.

The teacher mentioned in the opening example was forty years old and single. I wonder how many other middle-aged, single teachers who get close to their students in very good ways came under suspicion in some people's minds. When one or two police officers are suspended after charges of unnecessary force, how many other officers—even if they're tough cops in *good* ways—are suspected to be brutes if given the chance? If a summer camp leader is found to have abused a child, does that mean any adult youth worker who puts his or her arm around a child is very likely a sex offender?

Suspecting people of immoral behavior simply because they fit a certain profile is wrong. It can make us suspicious of almost everybody for one reason or another. If two little old ladies steal money from a church bingo, does that mean you should lock up all your cash and valuables when Grandma and a couple of her friends come to your house?

When the wrongdoer is someone we know well and once admired, perhaps even been close to, our thoughts go scattering like a set of billiard balls after they've been solidly hit with the cue ball. We search for a revised way of looking at that person and how we feel about him or her.

At first, it seems like there are two possibilities. (1) In spite of outward appearances, this was simply a bad person. We, along with many others, have been fooled by those appearances. (2) This was a person with many good qualities, who did many wonderful things but who also had a "tragic flaw," as it's called in literature (Macbeth's ambition to power, for example). He or she has a weakness that, when given in to, led to the actions that are now the scandal.

Well…both explanations are possible. Some people— there's no way of telling how many, but certainly some— deliberately and freely embrace evil and are then controlled by it and operate from it. It's difficult to explain many events of history in any other way. And others are obviously good—perhaps in many ways positively wonderful—people with a "tragic flaw." Maybe there are degrees in between; I don't know. In any case, that person needs prayer.

A prayer for such a person is difficult if he or she truly seems to have embraced evil and deliberately chosen to do very bad things. At the same time, who could need prayer more? Praying for such a person is clearly an act of loving someone who's tough to love. There's no emotional reward as there is in praying for someone for whom we feel sympathy or even admiration in spite of his or her mistakes.

If the person seems to fit the "tragic flaw" description, remember that all the genuinely good things about that person are still true and valid. If the wrong behavior has become public, that person probably thinks that all the good things about him or her have been wiped out or reduced to nothing…at least in people's minds—which might indeed be the case. That may be the most difficult consequence of all to deal with—more painful than a huge fine, loss of position, or even a jail sentence.

It's a sinful world, full of moral mistakes. But we shouldn't lower our own standards when someone we admire has lowered his or hers, whether frequently or on a single occasion. We shouldn't automatically see that person as a total moral garbage pit. We shouldn't become immediately suspicious of everyone who fits a similar profile of age, occupation, interests, or ambitions.

An old Russian spiritual proverb says, "Every saint has a past, and every sinner a future." In one way or another, that applies to all of us.

Words From the Word

God blessed Noah and his sons.

Genesis 9:1

Noah…was the first to plant a vineyard. He drank some of the wine and became drunk and he lay uncovered in his tent. Then Shem and Japheth took a garment, laid it on both their shoulders, and walked backward and covered the nakedness of their father.

Genesis 9:20–21; 23

Show yourself in all respects a model of good works.

Titus 2:7

Other Voices

Lilies that fester smell far worse than weeds.

Shakespeare

There is so much good in the worst of us, and so much bad in the best of us, that it hardly becomes any of us to talk about the rest of us.

Anonymous

Bottom Line

Scandal happens because people, even good people, make moral mistakes, sometimes very big ones. We can't afford to let that make us sour about life, about ideals, or about what those people represented poorly. And we can't afford to let it lead us to lower our own standards of behavior.

TWELVE

WHEN SOMEONE'S PROBLEM IS GIVING YOU A PROBLEM

> The human spirit will endure sickness; but a broken spirit—who can bear?
>
> *Proverbs 18:14*

❧

I f you've seen *What's Eating Gilbert Grape?* you'll remember that *many* things are eating away at Gilbert— at his energy, resources, and hope. His father isn't around anymore. His mother and his younger brother are afflicted with very different but serious conditions that affect not just themselves but other people, especially Gilbert, who basically has to take care of the family, even though it's not supposed to be his role.

Gilbert Grape is being drained, exhausted, and used up —and not by bad people, although some people in his life are pretty selfish. He's being used up mostly by good people. They require huge amounts of time and emotional energy that most people Gilbert's age put into planning and building their own adult lives. No one else supports or helps him in carrying out the unusual responsibilities that life has dealt him.

If you're never in a "Gilbert Grape situation," consider yourself fortunate because it's one of the toughest things young people have to deal with. It means someone in your family or someone close to you is afflicted with a significant disorder. It might be physical, emotional, or mental. Sometimes all three are present in the same condition. The situation significantly affects your life, drains your energy, causes you worry, and frequently colors the day gray.

If it seems that the person is responsible for causing his or her condition, or for remaining in it, that makes you angry. Alcoholism and other addictions, such as gambling, can appear that way. It seems to you that if the drinker or the gambler would grow some guts, use some will power, and decide what's really important and valuable (you, for example, rather than beer or slot machines), life would be a lot better and a lot fairer.

When that doesn't happen, you feel hurt and angry that a thing, a thrill of some kind, seems to be more important to the person than you are. You feel that way even though you may have heard that addictions like alcoholism are diseases over which a person, once he or she gets there, has very little control. You hear that people with serious addictions need specialized, professional help, and you believe that, but it still seems like the addicted person in your life should realize his or her condition and ask for the help.

Depression is equally difficult to deal with. You certainly can't accuse the depressed person of choosing a thrill over you and a normal life because he or she spends a great deal of time feeling miserable and emotionally paralyzed. Again, you may have heard and believe that this is a condition over which a person has little or no control. But that doesn't help a lot when the person is spreading leaden gloom over the household. You feel like screaming that there *are* some things going *right,* and that he or she just might spend a few seconds thinking about them. Sometimes you're not sure whom to be angry with.

Sometimes the disorder is just a really rotten bad break clearly and totally beyond his or her control. Cancer, a stroke, Alzheimer's disease, or any other physical condition which partially or largely disables the person. You can't cast blame there. Nevertheless, it affects your life too. As with Gilbert Grape, it puts limitations on the time you'd like to spend and need to spend developing your own life. Again, you're not certain whom to be angry with. The most common targets are life in general, everybody in general, and God.

Admitting this anger and dealing with it is not easy or pleasant. So, frequently some "coping mechanisms" (ways to make life livable or seem livable) swing into play. Now there are good coping mechanisms and bad ones. But one in particular is bad—denial. "Everything is fine"; or "There's a problem, but it doesn't bother me," which is just a variation of the first. Both the above are like, "Coach, my ankle isn't really sprained even if it is red and twice its normal size, and besides, even if it *is* sprained, I can play on it just fine."

Denial is like taking painkillers to soothe that sprained ankle. They may dull or even temporarily ease the pain, but you've still got a sprained ankle that will only get worse.

More than a few times I've talked with students who were dealing with a family problem and I've said, "That must hurt"—and heard the reply, "Not really. It doesn't bother me." Sometimes I would respond, "Then why are we talking about it," and sometimes I would be a little more blunt, "You're lying."

If denial doesn't work, what does? The opposite—accepting the truth. So, the first step is the same as in any of the classic recovery programs, such as Alcoholics Anonymous. If someone else's problem is affecting your life, you need to admit this to yourself.

Then spend some time identifying the feelings that you've been carrying around. It's okay to start with, "It makes me feel bad," but go beyond that generality to the specifics. Some possibilities include angry, resentful, cheated out of a normal life, and hopeless or powerless to change anything. Identifying those specific feelings is important. You have to know what's going on before you can deal with it. It's like admitting, "I have a sharp, stabbing pain in my right side every time I run," instead of just saying, "I don't feel so good."

Along the way, you need to avoid two demons that love to prey on a situation like this.

Demon # 1: Guilt. Guilt can make you feel that somehow you're the cause, or one of the causes, of someone else's addictive behavior. The addicted person may deliberately try to sow the seeds of guilt or fertilize them in some way. If you buy it, you may end up thinking that if you were a better, more productive, easier-to-deal-with teen or young adult, the other person would not have his or her problem.

But in the case of genuine addiction or depression, this is as far from the truth as you can get. Support groups for people with a compulsive person in their lives often cite the "three C's:" You didn't *cause* the problem; you can't *control* the problem; you can't *cure* the problem. That may sound discouraging, but it's also freeing.

Second, if the afflicted person's problem is something that prompts pity or sympathy (a serious, perhaps terminal disease, for example), it's easy to feel a little guilty for not having the same suffering, or at least some kind of suffering. You can actually feel a little guilty for wanting a life or for genuinely enjoying the fun parts of the life you do have. This does nobody any good—neither you nor the person you care about.

Demon # 2: Excuses. Having a problem—including the problem of dealing with someone else's problem—always brings the temptation to use it as an excuse for behavior that creates more problems. It can be as obvious as "I have to drink a little myself in order to put up with Mom's drinking" or "If Dad does it, why shouldn't I?" Or it can be subtle and hardly put into words at all, such as not working very hard at school because life in general feels so unrewarding.

Underlying the excuse, whether it's obvious or faint, is what you really mean to say: "I need to have a life. I need to give myself a break, some pleasure, some unwinding." And that's true. But the break, the pleasure, the unwinding need to be genuine and healthy things, not something that gives you the same problem, a similar problem, or *any* kind of problem.

Psychologists call this defense mechanism "acting out," a fancy term that means "fooling around and using somebody else's problem as an excuse for doing so."

Acting out can be almost anything: literally copying someone's negative behavior; getting involved in trouble at school or even with the law; having meaningless, casual sex; or (very commonly) avoiding responsibilities. ("How can anybody expect me to concentrate and accomplish anything when I have all this #%$&@!! to put up with?")

If you have a situation like those we've described to cope with, don't try to do it that way. It's not coping; it's spraying destructive painkillers. Your life may be different from that of many of your peers (although more of them than you realize may share a similar situation). But different does not mean doomed, it's not a synonym for shoddy, and it does not *have* to mean usually miserable or unproductive.

Through all this, God may appear deaf. You know in your head that this isn't true, but you pray over the situation and nothing seems to change. The most common kind of prayer, however, is "Dear God, *please change Dad/Mom/whoever/whatever,*" or something very close to that. Since that hasn't happened, it looks like God is deaf or doesn't care or somehow isn't even able to do anything in spite of being God.

Let go of the "Dear God, please change _____" prayer and begin praying for guidance to be shown what to do, how to bear up. Repeat this prayer many times— not because it takes a while to get God's attention, or because God demands a large amount of "prayer prepayment" before he agrees to do anything, but because it takes time for God's reply to get through to us. *We're* the ones who need frequent and extended times of prayer so that we can absorb and understand God's answer. Leave *lots* of time for listening, which is the part of prayer that we usually leave out.

You might also enlist the help of some saints who had significant parental problems. Saint Francis of Assisi's father locked him in a room and bad-mouthed him to everyone. Saint Thomas Aquinas' parents locked him in a tower, and Saint Catherine of Siena's family made her their household servant.

Is it ever possible to confront the person with the problem who is giving you a problem? Sure. Obviously, you won't do this if the other's problem is cancer or some other out-of-control disease that cannot be helped. But if it's a condition that *could* be remedied...? Sure. It's a risk. It may or may not work well, and it probably won't start an instant and dramatic turnaround, but it's worth a shot.

The *when*, the *where*, and the *how* are extremely important—crucial, in fact.

When. Choose a time when the person is not under the immediate influence of the problem. If he or she is drunk or on the way to getting there, that's a really bad time to talk about drinking. So is hangover time. If he or she is feverishly in the middle of a project, that's a bad time to talk about working too much. Choose a neutral time, a time when things are going relatively well. Pray over the timing; you don't have to do this alone, you know.

Where. Choose a place where the person won't feel embarrassed or put on the spot in front of others (unless you and your siblings are doing this as a group). An embarrassing public confrontation is almost certain to backfire.

How. The tone of what you say should be as caring and loving as you can make it, rather than resentful and accusing. Perhaps begin with a compliment and some good memories of past times. Say what you admire and mean it. If you can't find anything to admire, probably because you're angry, look further. Few people are so awful that you cannot find any good in them.

This is not cheap greasing the surface or phony, initial sucking up—unless you mean it that way. It's simply working with human nature. You're about to say something the other person may misinterpret—namely, that you think he or she is a bad person. You need to make it known that you think he or she is a *good* person...who needs to change something for everyone's benefit, including his or her own.

In bringing up the problem, stress that you're concerned or worried about him or her. Maybe eventually you have to say, "I resent the way you act," but that will be much easier to hear if "I really care about you" comes first.

State as calmly as you can how the person's behavior makes you feel. Psychologists call this an "I-message," which works better because it focuses on the *effects* of the person's *behavior*. That's very different from stating what kind of *person* he or she is.

As before, try to be very specific, as opposed to "it makes me feel bad." Possibilities include angry, hurt, cheated, upset, lost, left out, used, unimportant, ignored, confused, put down, disappointed, unappreciated, embarrassed, discouraged, worried, and even hopeless.

"Dad, you know what? You're an alcoholic and the only thing you care about is getting hammered; you don't give a damn about your family!" Oh, wow…guaranteed to start an absolute war.

"Dad, when you go through eight or ten beers in an evening and get confused and irritable and sloppy talking, I feel really embarrassed for you. I feel like I don't count in your life anymore, and I'm really worried." Now we're focused on the facts and the feelings, not on a general accusation.

In *any* confrontation, three words are toxic, deadly, and therefore similarly guaranteed to start a war: *always, never,* and *only.*

"You *always* ruin everything." "You *never* care about me or anyone else." "The *only* thing that matters to you is your job."

These are battle-starters because they're extremely big accusations, and most of the time they really are untrue and therefore unfair. A parent, for example, may indeed be drinking or working way too much—but that really isn't exactly the same as literally never caring about anyone.

When someone hears a negative "always" or "never" or "only" statement about him or herself, he or she immediately thinks, "Wait—that's just not true!" and begins creating a defense against the accusation. From that point on, the conversation centers on whether or not that huge *accusation* is true and supportable by evidence. The *behavior*—which was supposed to be the topic—gets lost.

I don't believe Gilbert Grape ever said, "Hey, I don't deserve this!" but people in his situation certainly think and feel it, including you at times if you're in a Gilbert Grape situation. You're right, you don't. And nobody does. Nobody *deserves* anything bad. Nobody *deserves* to be weighed down by anybody else's imperfections. And nobody will…in heaven. But we're not there yet. In the meantime, we have to deal with such situations when they happen here on earth.

You can choose souring resentment, paralyzing self-pity, or self-destructive acting out. Or you can choose to try your best to understand the situation and act as intelligently and charitably as possible, with a legitimate view to your own best interests and future. You can decide that someone else's problem is not going to doom your future or shove your present into a garbage pit. You can choose to be a victim or a survivor.

Choosing to be a victim is easy. It takes no effort. You just let yourself be carried helplessly down the river toward the deadly waterfall. Choosing to be a survivor is work. But it works.

Words From the Word

I loathe my life; I will give free utterance to my complaint; I will speak in the bitterness of my soul.

Job 10:1 (not the end of the story!)

The Lord blessed the latter days of Job more than his beginning.

Job 42:12 (the end of the story)

Other Voices

Forgiving those who hurt us is the key to personal peace.

G. Weatherly

What poison is to food, self-pity is to life.

Oliver C. Wilson

Bottom Line

Having your life affected by someone else's serious problem is unfair. Dealing with it is difficult. You can choose to let that situation defeat and even doom you, or you can choose to prevail over it and become who you were meant to be anyway. Ask God for help. Often. Really often. And listen.

THIRTEEN

WHEN A PARENT IS OUT OF WORK

Now hope that is seen is not hope. For who hopes for what is seen? But if we hope for what we do not see, we wait for it with patience.

Romans 8:24–25

❦

Chances are you didn't notice the foundation of your house or apartment building when you came home today. (If one of your parents works in construction, you may even know how to frame and pour a foundation. For the rest of us, it's that mostly underground wall of concrete that looks pretty important to the rest of the building—and is.)

Imagine that you arrive home one day and find that one side of the foundation has buckled, caved in, and sunk several inches. Imagine further that right now you have nowhere else to live.

The floor tilts. Cracks that weren't there yesterday appear in the walls and get wider day by day. The ceiling sags. It puts everyone on edge.

When a parent loses a job, it's somewhat like that. The family structure doesn't blow up, but it's put under a strain that tests everyone's strength and faith.

The real foundation of a family is the relationship and love between family members, not the size of a parent's paycheck. Nevertheless, a family needs shelter and enough money for food, clothing, and other necessities. When a parent, especially a single parent, loses a job, those things can feel and actually be kind of iffy.

If you find yourself in that situation, you can expect some of the reactions and feelings mentioned below. They're all normal and, by themselves, they're neither good nor bad. But like all feelings, depending on how they're handled, they can lead to things that *are* good or bad.

- *"It's no big deal" (denial).* When the body is badly injured, it goes into shock and tries to block out the pain. It's a defense against the damage. When the mind does that, as we've seen in other chapters, it's called "denial." It's a way of trying not to feel the seriousness of a situation. That reaction may be needed for a brief time, but it soon outlives its usefulness and needs to be discarded in favor of reality. Unless the family has a huge bank account in reserve, being out of work *is* a big deal.

- *Worry.* Unless you're very young, you know that losing a job doesn't eliminate the bills or reduce necessary expenses. The rent or the house payment is still due on the same day of the month, cereal still needs milk, and the car still needs gas.

Worry is a sign of being tuned in to reality. That awareness is good as long as it doesn't become a devouring monster that paralyzes you and prevents you (or gives you a convenient excuse) from fulfilling obligations that, like the family bills, are still there in your life. These are probably primarily school responsibilities.

- *Embarrassment.* We all want to feel that we're making it, and we want others to know that we are. Likewise, we want to feel, and want others to know, that our *family* is making it, even if we don't always get along with family members. When a parent loses a job, it's easy to feel that your family is somehow less respectable. It's even easier to think that others who know about the situation feel that way, although the chances are they really don't.

- *Depression.* We've noted before that depression is usually triggered by some kind of change and/ or loss. When a parent loses a job, both are involved.

  Schedules change. The unemployed parent is at home when others are accustomed to having some time and space by themselves. This has nothing to do with loving or not loving that person. Or—the opposite—the unemployed parent is out job-hunting and interviewing when he or she could normally be counted on to run the household and drive kids to and from soccer practice.

Loss of income leads to other losses. These may include biggies like an eagerly anticipated major vacation or plans to enroll in a very good (and expensive) college. They almost always include smaller losses, like being able to order a pizza on Saturday night.

- *Anger.* Anger can be a natural reaction to difficult change. In this situation, the anger can be directed at the parent's former employer, God, life in general, siblings who may not seem to understand and help as they should, classmates and peers who have well-employed parents and therefore a financially comfortable life, and even the unemployed parent.

- *Self-pity.* When a parent is out of work, it's easy to feel sorry for yourself, especially if you live in a neighborhood where some items are considered necessary even when they really aren't.

Peers have cell phones; you had to give yours up. Peers go to $55-a-ticket concerts and bring home $30 concert T-shirts; you stay home and watch old videos. Peers prepare for a major party with a $100+ trip to the mall; you search your closet for something that attempts to look new.

You can adjust the occasions and the prices up or down depending on your situation and locality, but you get the idea.

Understanding your own feelings is one side of the coin. Understanding your parent's feelings is the other. They're similar, but the parent's version is colored by his or her experience and sense of responsibility as leader and provider.

The parent's anger will be intensified if he or she has spent several years on the job and put great effort into it. If *you* feel the situation is unfair, your parent is feeling the same thing many times more.

Recall the times you were really angry over something unfair in your life. Recall how you dealt with it, including the times you didn't deal with it very well, and it spilled over into other places and onto other people. If your parent is irritable, try to see through that and sympathize with his or her situation. And remember that he or she has done this for you many times. (Remember all the times you came home foul-tempered because a math test was, in your opinion, seriously unfair?)

You're usually nervous about starting something new, like trying out for a team or a school play or the student council or a job. But you don't consider it unfair. It doesn't feel unnatural. It goes with the territory of being young and, in many areas, a beginner. You expect that. It's the way life works.

It's not the same for a parent who is thirty-five, forty-five, fifty or more, and who is suddenly forced to find a new workplace where he or she will again be either a genuine beginner, or at least "the new kid."

If the job search drags on for several weeks or months,

it can eat away at a parent's self-esteem. It's true that we're human *beings,* not human *doings,* and a person is infinitely lovable in God's eyes just because he or she exists. At the same time, it's very hard, especially for an adult, to completely separate what he or she *does* from his or her feeling of worth. An unemployed parent may feel that he or she is not doing anything productive, and therefore not worth much.

Getting *some* kind of a job may not be a problem. But finding a job that (1) fits one's background, skills, and interests; and (2) brings in the salary the family needs—that's often a very different matter. It's especially true for an adult who has lost a job in a very particular or specialized field. Someone who has spent twenty years as an architect, for example, does not have the experience to manage an office or a restaurant. Be sympathetic if a parent feels nervous or even scared about changing careers and going to interviews in what feels like a foreign land.

It's your parent's responsibility to work hard at finding a job. But you're an important part of the endurance process at home. If you're an older teen, you may be the family's needed messiah. Now that probably sounds very strange for this situation, but it isn't. The Hebrew word *messiah* means "anointed," just as the Greek word *Christos* does, and "anointed" means something like "chosen for a mission." Jesus, of course, was *THE* Messiah with the mission of saving the world. But each of us is a messiah at different times for different people. That's how God works.

In this case, your mission is helping your unemployed parent and your whole family through a difficult time. Looking at the situation as a mission you've been chosen for puts it in a much more pleasant light. Feeling that you have a purpose is much better than feeling deprived.

Above all, encourage your parent who's looking for a job. Let him or her know that he or she is still your hero, and that you're proud of him or her. Surprise your parent with a little gift, even something as small as a favorite candy bar. Remember that your parent did similar things for you many, many times. Now is a much-needed payback time.

On a practical, nuts-and-bolts level, here are some things you can do to help the family through this difficult time. If you look at them in the right light, they can even be fun.

- *Adjust your own spending,* whether it's your personal money, or money that the family usually provides. If you usually spend several dollars in the school cafeteria, pack your lunch. Put your desires for new things on hold until family finances get stabilized. And do this with grace, class, and style—which basically means keeping quiet about it. ("You know, I'm not getting the new ___ I was looking forward to; I hope this helps" kind of spoils it.)
- *Share your earnings.* If you work, pick up the tab for milk and bread at the store, or for a younger sibling's treat after a soccer game. Fill

the car's gas tank now and then. Pay for the video rental. With a little imagination, you'll find a dozen ways to give the family finances a little help without crippling your own.

- *Look for ways to economize.* Turn off lights and appliances that aren't being used, no matter who left them on. Tape TV shows rather than renting videos or DVD's. Make meals rather than eating out. Learn to drink water or powdered drinks rather than buying soda in cans or 2-liter containers. Combine errands to make one trip rather than three. Limit Internet and cell-phone time. If a piece of clothing can be worn another time without being washed (which means without looking dirty or smelling nasty), hang it up rather than automatically throwing it in the laundry pile. If, like many of us, you consume chips by the handful, try eating one at a time and really savoring the taste. You may find yourself eating fewer chips and actually enjoying them more.

- *Look for ways to lighten things up,* especially if the situation is tense and patience is in short supply. Be the peacemaker, even when things affect you, and try never to be a peace breaker. Take charge of younger siblings or of housework when your parent is feeling down or trying to work on possible job opportunities.

When a parent is out of work, and financial worries set in, a tense gloom can settle over a household. The situation seems so unfair when the parent desperately wants to work but cannot find anything suitable. It can be hard for the family to feel that God cares, particularly if everyone has been praying that a decent job will open up and so far, none have. (Along with continued, persevering prayer to God, you might also enlist the help of Saint Joseph, the patron saint of workers, who had to start over more than once in his lifetime.)

For a teen, it means trying to carry on all the tasks of school and growing up while living in a household where, in a sense, the floor tilts, the ceiling sags, and ominous cracks appear in the walls. It's a very tough situation, a very big test of faith, and no easy way out. But deliberately trying to make things easier for the others in your household is probably the best way to make things easier for yourself. That makes it a double winner.

Words From the Word

And can any of you by worrying add a single hour to your span of life?

Matthew 6:27

I consider that the sufferings of this present time are not worth comparing with the glory about to be revealed to us.

Romans 8:18

Other Voices

The human spirit is stronger than anything that can happen to it.

George C. Scott

Courage mounteth with occasion.

William Shakespeare

Bottom Line

A parent's unemployment can make things tense in a household, puts a strain on family relationships, and even tests faith. Rather than seeing yourself as a secondary victim, try to be a builder of peace and hope.

EPILOGUE

"Thank you for calling Pizza World, my name is Alice, will this be for pickup or delivery?"

"Are you still including shriveled, greasy, grotty bologna and rancid chicken gristles?"

"I'm sorry, that was last month's promotion. This month we have slimy turkey fat and rotting fish tails. Will this be for pickup or delivery?"

"Actually, neither. I just want to make a statement."

"There's also a free side order of hyper salted pork rinds. Will this be for pickup or delivery?"

"Alice, I don't want your pizza. I just want to make a statement."

"Will your statement be for pickup or delivery?"

"I'll deliver it right now. See, I would *never* deliberately, knowingly order a pizza with all that nasty stuff on it. But I just want you to know that the other day, somebody sent me one."

"That was very nice of them."

"Matter of opinion. Point is, I was really hungry, and there wasn't much else around to eat. I want you to know that I got through it. I survived. I was able to pick my way through the greasy, grotty bologna and concentrate on the other stuff, and even when I got a piece of the grotty bologna in me, my taste buds toughed it out. It wasn't fun, but I survived."

"You've changed your mind! Will your order be for pickup or delivery?"

"Neither. I'm just saying that if—and I hope it never happens—but *if* for some reason I ever have to survive another Pizza World special, I can do it."

"That's good news. And you can prove it right now. As I said, this month's promotion is—"

"No pickup. No delivery."

"And there's a free side order—"

"Good-bye, Alice."

Words From the Word

You then, my child, be strong in the grace that is in Christ Jesus.

2 Timothy 2:1

Other Voices

We have what we seek. It is there all the time, and if we give it time, it will make itself known to us.

Thomas Merton

Pain is never permanent.

Saint Teresa of Ávila

There ain't no cloud so thick that the sun ain't shinin' on the other side.

"Rattlesnake," 1870s mountain man